THE PLAGUE STORY AND OTHER ESSAYS

THE PLAGUE STORY AND OTHER ESSAYS

Re-evaluating the Coronavirus Narrative

SIMON SHERIDAN

Simon Sheridan

CONTENTS

Preface: Why you shouldn't believe a word I say

The reader should know upfront that I am completely unqualified to speak about pretty much every topic in this book. I am not an epidemiologist, an infectious disease specialist, a biologist, a microbiologist, a virologist, an immunologist, a mathematician, a statistician, a mathematical epidemiologist, an epidemiological mathematician, a doctor, a nurse, a nurse's aide, a public health bureaucrat, an academic, an economist, a sociologist, a risk analyst, a politician, a journalist, a soldier, a policeman, a pundit, a podcaster, an op-ed writer, a thought leader, a content creator, an advertising executive, a marketing expert, a public relations specialist, a funeral director, a grief counsellor, a psychotherapist, a priest, a butcher, a baker or a candlestick maker.

There is an idea that is very fashionable these days that only experts may talk about things. One of the most poignant examples of that attitude I have seen was a video where one of my favourite scientists, Kary Mullis, was addressing an audience at a university in the USA. Mullis, a classic iconoclast in the Feynman tradition, inevitably gave a dissenting opinion about some topic or other. A student arose from the audience during question time and, rather than disagree about the content of what Mullis had said, simply told him he was not qualified to speak. He was not an expert in that field and shouldn't be talking about it.

This was naturally anathema to Mullis who told the man that he was perfectly capable of making arguments about whatever subject he liked. But it was quite clear that many others in the audience agreed with the student. For a second, it seemed that a mob might form against a Nobel Prize winner for science for talking about, well, science.

Let me reiterate: I am not qualified. I am not even a Nobel Prize winner. If you think these things disqualify me from speaking, you should stop reading right now.

That a blind faith in the experts is a big part of what caused the corona event is a central thesis of this book. The problems brought about by that blind faith have already been pointed out by a number of thinkers. One of my favourites is Gerald Weinberg and his book *General Systems Thinking*. It explains in detail the kinds of errors that experts get into and how to avoid them. The antidote to an expert is a generalist (aka a layperson). It is not a matter of one or the other perspective being 'correct', it is that they are complementary. There are things that generalists can see that experts cannot. Of course, in theory there is no reason why an individual can't be both an expert and a generalist but it just seems to be that our society produces mostly experts who are not also generalists. Most likely this is because of the increasing specialisation within the science and technology fields. The sheer volume of work produced now means that people tend to limit themselves to a microscopic area of study to the exclusion of broader scientific and social concerns. This has led to a kind of hyper-expertise which has created an imbalance in our society. Such an imbalance is partly what has driven the corona event.

One of the ways to be a generalist and avoid the errors of the expert is precisely not to get bogged down in details. This doesn't mean that drilling down into the minutiae isn't necessary sometimes, just that you must always be able to come up for air and incorporate what you found into a bigger picture. Like a deep-sea diver, you have to keep a connection back to the surface lest you disappear forever into the depths. Another way to avoid error in complex domains is to have as many different models as you can. When dealing with complexity, you simply cannot put all your eggs in one basket. It is better to know the basics in ten different domains than to know everything about one. The systems thinking outlined by Weinberg set itself the seemingly modest task of avoiding error. Those looking for heroism and grandiose, world-changing schemes will not find much inspiration in it. But egotism has always been a hindrance when it to comes to science and to my mind one of the defining features of the corona event is hubris. Belief in experts seems to go hand-in-hand with believing that we know more than we really do. In fact, as we will see throughout this book, expertise often leads to a kind of megalomania. Systems thinking is an antidote to such tendencies.

If these ideas are new to you, I invite you to use this book to judge their worth. It is the work of a non-expert, an amateur, a generalist. It is written in the spirit of science as defined by Richard Feynman as 'the belief in the ignorance of experts.' It contains no definitive answers but best guesses. I believe that in the real world, with all its irreducible complexity, that is all we can hope for. We must avoid large errors so that we can keep making our best guesses and through them to keep reaching forward into the unknown to see what we might find.

I hope you find something here. I guess that you will.

Preface 2: Why you should listen to what I say

Having hopefully scared off the fundamentalists in the first preface, let me now outline why I wrote this book and why I believe my perspective will be of value to the reader.

Firstly, I did postgraduate work in linguistics and worked briefly as a linguist following my studies. So, I have seen the inside of academia and also understand broadly how science works both as a discipline and organisationally in the modern world.

Secondly, I have worked for more than a decade in what I am calling in this book the technocracy. But my role has been that of a generalist rather than an expert. Specifically, I am a software tester. I got the job despite having no experience or qualifications. All I knew about coding was what I had learned in high school and growing up, which was not much. That might sound strange to people who would probably assume that the best person to test things is somebody who understands the domain. But, in the world of software testing it was understood, at least in some circles, that there is a perspective that a non-expert brings that is both valuable and also very unlikely to be found in the expert. This equates to a distinction between white box and black box testing and has intellectual ties to the systems thinking and cybernetics movements of the 20th century. It was in this job that I first learned about Gerald Weinberg who I mentioned in the last chapter as his theories provided the justification for the value of black box testing among other things.

Therefore, the critiques of the technocracy that I will make and reference in this book are born out of practical experience. I have seen first-hand the kinds of errors and misunderstandings that happen in technical work. Oftentimes, these errors are related to a high-level ideology that goes back to the last 19th and early 20th century and is based on a naïve optimism about how science and technology could re-shape the world for the benefit of all. Of course, science and technology can and has done that, but those who subscribe to the ideology have a habit of ignoring the negative side effects and outright failures of science and technology. In my job as a software tester, it was my responsibility to point out error on a daily basis and so I know also the psychological and emotional reasons why people like to imagine that everything is fine. Much of the time an 'error' is really a miscommunication. Thus, one of the most obvious ways to avoid error is to make communication as effortless as possible allowing people to clarify their own understanding by asking questions and challenging assumptions. Where this communication doesn't happen, things simply don't work in any domain where there is a level of complexity involved.

Finally, I am also a storywriter. I have three novels to my name as well as a number of short stories. I understand the power of stories in both the structural and technical sense. In my professional life, work is often broken up into things called 'stories' because it is understood that humans are storytelling animals and it is simply a convenient way for us to understand things. One of the surest ways to look for misunderstanding is to look at the stories different groups and individuals are telling themselves and how they differ from the stories others are telling. The core of this book is identifying the dominant narrative we have been using during the corona event – the plague story. Along the way we will touch on a number of the other stories and myths that form the backbone of modern western society.

What sort of work is this book? It is part history, part anthropology, part sociology, part psychology, part literary analysis. The list could go on. In short, it takes a multi-disciplinary approach. For that reason, I think of it as inspired by systems theory and cybernetics as both of those movements were about incorporating concepts from across disciplines and looking for common themes, patterns and connections. I like to imagine that the corona event is an object and we are picking it up, turning it around and looking at it from different angles. Systems thinking is all about having many different lenses with which to view something. In this book I will invoke a literary lens, a history lens, a scientific lens, an economic lens, a cultural and psychological lens and others. The aim is to try and place the corona event in a larger context so that we might better understand it. This book started life as a series of essays and it remains in that form. Each chapter is a relatively self-contained perspective on the corona event.

Nevertheless, the book does contain a unified perspective and to outline what that is it might help to quickly clarify upfront some core concepts I will use throughout the book.

I draw a distinction between science and technocracy. Technocracy was an actual political movement early in the 20th century which argued that scientists and technicians should run society according to 'science' (whatever that really means). The technocracy movement didn't last long as a political force. Nevertheless, the corona event represents a form of technocracy. States of emergency were declared which gave actual political power to public health bureaucrats. Those bureaucrats were in touch with another technocratic organisation: the World Health Organisation. The assumption was that the WHO and the public health bureaucracy have been using 'science' to guide public policy decisions.

I define 'science' using Richard Feynman's definition as 'belief in the ignorance of experts' both because I believe that to be a proper definition of the spirit of science and also because it draws into stark contrast the problems with technocracy. *Live* science almost always features multiple explanatory frameworks that account for the facts in different ways. Disagreement and argument is common, in fact desirable, in science. But the technocracy is about action. The pretence that the technocracy is based on science therefore ignores the fact that some science is always getting deliberately filtered out of any real world decisions.

We can see that this definition of science and technocracy are kind of mutually exclusive. If science is belief in the ignorance of experts it follows that the idea of putting them in charge is the equivalent of putting the ignorant in charge (although arguably this is what we already do in modern democracy!). I call the belief that putting the experts in charge is a good idea *high modernist ideology*, a concept taken from James C. Scott's excellent book *Seeing Like a State*. High modernist ideology implies a simplified and naïve understanding of science; the kind of understanding that washes away the ambiguities of science and pretends that science can indeed solve all our problems. This ideology has been at play throughout the corona event whenever a politician, technocrat, journalist or an individual stated or implied that we must believe exclusively and unconditionally in the 'science' or the 'experts'. This has been a common way to shut down debate during the corona event including dissenting opinions from actual scientists.

Is it possible to be both a true scientist and a technocrat? I don't believe so. In practice, technocracy filters out all science that cannot be used for political purposes. One way this happens is to tie scientific research to funding sources that are pursuing a political agenda. This is true of most scientific research in the modern world and contrasts strongly with the age of heroic science where the great scientists were usually independent actors. More on this later on the book.

I will use the phrase *heroic materialism* to denote the founding and primary ethos of modern western culture. The term is taken from the title of the last episode of Kenneth Clark's 1969 television series *Civilisation*. It refers mostly to the industrial revolution but also implies the myth of progress and the concept of heroic science. More on this later, as well.

These concepts define the background of our society and culture that I believe are most relevant to the corona event. They form the kind of subconscious cultural glue that has united the scientists, technocrats, politicians, the media and the public. In this book I will bring them into the light and evaluate the role they played.

One final note before we get started. With this book I have limited myself to areas where I feel I have something to say that is worth hearing. As a result, I have deliberately left out factors that are relevant to what has happened. It's worth highlighting two of those. Firstly, the political machinations behind corona, in particular the lobby groups and financial interests that revolve around the business of modern medicine and the biomedical sciences. I don't have any special access to the players in that game and so I made a decision not to pursue that angle. Secondly, in-depth analysis of both the individual and group psychology that got us into the corona event and the on-going psychological fallout. It seems quite clear to me that for many people the corona event is a mass hysteria in the technical sense of the term. There are also deep-seated fears about illness as well as culturally specific fears around viruses that have played a role. I don't have confidence that my thoughts in these areas would be anything more than speculation and so I decided to also forego this topic.

What this book *is* about is stories. As I will say time and time again, stories are what drive society. They are the link between politics and the public. The social and the psychological. The layperson and the expert.

"Those who tell the stories, rule society." – Plato

Introduction

Humans have a cognitive bias for linear functions. One of the ways in which this manifests is that we expect the magnitude of the cause and the magnitude of the effect to be equal. This expectation works well in everyday situations. For example, if you throw a rock, the more effort you put into the throw, the further the rock will travel. The larger the rock, the heavier it will weigh etc. Linear functions, or at least what we perceive as linear functions, form the basis for everyday life. Much of science education involves teaching the student to overcome this bias and understand alternative functions.

As the corona event unfolded, various experts, and even the Chancellor of Germany, who is, after all, a scientist by training, took to the media to remind us that pandemics need to be understood as exponential functions. We heard all about the R0, the doubling time of cases and the possibly explosive growth of infections. Nevertheless, most of the media presented the corona statistics as cumulative graphs rather than as log graphs. The cumulative graph, of course, looks linear thus satisfying our non-scientific preferences. It also looks scarier. A feature that appeals to the modern media.

So, we like linear functions. We expect the punishment to fit the crime. We demand an eye for an eye. We want a fair day's pay for a fair day's work. And when the government takes an extreme measure like locking down civil society, we expect that this must be in response to a genuine, highly dangerous threat. Only the most dire situation could justify such an unprecedented measure, we think to ourselves.

It was this expectation that formed my initial confusion about the corona event back when it was still mostly taking place in China. China had shut down an entire city on hours' notice. We heard stories about people being welded in their apartments and other extreme measures. The assumption would be that this virus must be super deadly. But even in the early days of the pandemic, this didn't make a lot of sense. The statistics didn't look *that* bad. The fatality rate seemed to be between 1-2% and the deaths were mostly among the elderly. It looked like a bad flu virus. So, I started to look for other explanations. I started to wonder whether there wasn't some political crisis going on in China. Maybe a civil war was breaking out in Wuhan. Maybe it was the latest move in the US-China trade war. Or maybe the Chinese government was trying to cover up what really was a health emergency and the official statistics were wrong. It didn't make much sense and there were no answers from the Western media who, at least where I lived, gave very little coverage to the goings on in China.

Slowly, like green slime dripping down a wall, the virus leaked into our lives in the West.

By mid-March, it still didn't look *that* bad. Epidemiological reports based on the evidence available at that time were estimating around a 1% fatality rate that would likely fall by an order of magnitude because that's what always happens with respiratory viral pandemics. It was going to be bad but not astronomically bad. Probably a little worse than the influenza pandemic in 2017 that was estimated to have killed 1.25 million people worldwide. Western governments at the time seemed to agree with this diagnosis of the situation. Our leaders pushed back against a rising tide of fear that was being fed by an increasingly voracious media. They tried to reassure the public that the situation could be handled without the extreme measures seen in China. The PR battle lasted about two weeks. Then, seemingly in unison, western governments rolled over and we went into preparations for the lockdown. Neil Ferguson's doomsday model was splattered all over the media and other models were found that predicted all kinds of awful outcomes. From that point right up until now there was nothing but wall-to-wall fear mongering in the media. The cool, calm, objective voices of the epidemiologists were drowned out by a growing tide of hysteria.

This period in February and March was the crucial moment in the corona event and will form the cornerstone of my analysis. We had a choice between two competing stories about what was going on: 1) the flu story; 2) what I am calling *the plague story* (aka pandemic). In my analysis, western governments tried to guide the public towards the flu story but they lost that battle and we entered into a plague story which is where we still are at the time of writing (September 2020). This book is about what that story is and why we got into it.

There a number of assumptions in my analysis that the reader may or may not share so I will outline them now for clarity:-

1. I believe that, for all our modern science, human nature has not changed in a long time
2. Part of human nature is that we orient ourselves to the world through stories. This is an especially important point in modern societies where we tell ourselves (the story!) that we don't believe in stories; we believe in science
3. As part of our nature as social animals, we bias towards conformity with others. This manifests in ideas such as social proof, groupthink and in extreme cases, mass hysteria
4. In the era of the internet and especially social media, the telling of a story and the associated social processes can take place almost instantly around the globe

None of this is good or bad in itself. In fact, our ability to coordinate with each other is arguably one of the things which conferred significant evolutionary benefit on the human species. What is a problem in modern society is that we deny these things in both a factual and a moral sense. We believe that we are scientific. We believe we are rational. We believe that progress has lifted us beyond our ancestors not just in a technological sense but in a moral sense. We think our beliefs about the world are based on science and not on stories. We think we are individuals who can think for ourselves independent of the beliefs of those around us. We may be one or all of these things. I simply make the point that we are also still just humans. Still subject to and at risk of being overcome by our emotions. Still taking our cues from others. And, most importantly for the purposes of this book, still storytellers. That is not a bad thing. Quite the opposite. Stories are an incredible technology that allow a compression of meaning that is as good as magic. What is important is to know that you are telling yourself a story and what story you are telling yourself. We have been telling ourselves a story whereby the corona event is a plague story. We started along the path into the plague story when the WHO's early warning system went off back in January. When western governments went into lockdown in March, we entered the plague story for real. At time of writing, we are still in the middle of the plague story and we don't know how to get out of it. How we eventually do get out of the story is anybody's guess at this point but until we do we are going to be in limbo. That's because societies run on stories. Not on facts. Not on 'science'. Not on risk analysis.

One of the stories we tell ourselves in modern society is that we are above stories. That's not true. We are human beings and we work with stories. We need to be aware of the stories we are telling ourselves so that we can interrogate them, make sure they reflect reality and, if necessary, look for better ones. In the next chapter, we'll begin our interrogation of the story we have been telling ourselves about the corona event: *the plague story*.

Chapter 1: The Plague Story

Stories matter. Even in our modern, scientific, hi-tech world, stories still function as the primary way that we give our life and our world meaning. As a storywriter myself, I am very well acquainted with the underlying structure of stories in the western tradition. Coming up with a story that isn't cliched is a difficult task and one that is failed by many writers. We've all had the dreary experience of knowing in advance what is going to happen in a movie or a book. The job of a good storyteller is to hide the underlying structure from the listener or reader so that they don't know what's coming. The underlying structure of stories is similar to the structure of grammar; they determine functional and semantic roles. That is why sometimes you know what somebody is going to say before they've even said it. You have intuited the structure of the sentence or story and this structure limits the options available. With enough knowledge of your conversation partner, their worldview and habits of speech it is not that hard to guess what they are going to say.

An example of how story structure can guide understanding can be seen from how some segments of the Christian community have had a discussion of whether the corona event represents the 'end times' plague that is predicted in the Bible. That might sound ridiculous to us who don't share the underlying assumptions of that community. Nevertheless, for them it is a real issue and the reason it is an issue is because, within their interpretation of the Bible, there is a part about an end times plague. There is a gap in the story structure waiting to be filled.

This *filling in the gaps* is not limited to stories; it goes to very fundamental levels of human perception. For example, in the visual field, the amount the eye is actually 'seeing' at any one time is very small. The brain fills in the rest. The way in which the brain does that *filling in* is subject to certain rules and we can play around with those rules to construct optical illusions which trick us into *seeing* something that is not really there. A similar thing can be done with audio perception where the bass frequencies can be completely removed from a signal but the listener can still determine the bass frequency from the overall audio pattern. Perhaps they will even 'hear' the bass.

Just like you can speak a language without having any analytical understanding of its grammar, you can understand or create a story without knowing the underlying structure. It's also possible, indeed normal, to not even be aware of the stories you are using just like you are not aware of the rules of grammar when you speak. Most of the stories we use to guide our understanding of the world are subconscious and this leads to a great deal of useless disagreement between people who think they are arguing about the details of such and such a thing when in reality they are both using different stories to explain what is going on. Most of us would be familiar with the experience of having a romantic relationship or close friendship break up and how we marvel at the fact that we could have been so blind about the other person. We assumed we were sharing the same story about what was happening but it turned out that was not the case. We were bickering over details without getting to the root of the problem.

The romantic relationship metaphor works quite nicely to elucidate this point. Let's say there are two stories that might be at play: the fling story and the life partner story. Once upon a time in western culture, as in most cultures, the life partner story was heavily regimented. There was a series of formal steps involved and there was never any doubt that you were in that story. But in the modern west we have blurred the boundaries so that it is now possible, even likely, for there to be confusion on the matter. Let's imagine a situation where the man thinks he is in a fling story while the woman think she is in a life partner story. The woman might suggest activities in line with the life partner story. For example, a date on Valentine's Day, an extended holiday or a meeting with her parents. If the man agrees to all of these, especially the last one, then he has fulfilled elements of the life partner story. If he were then to turn around and say that he thought they were just having a fling, the woman could rightly accuse him of having led her on which really means he participated willingly in the elements of that story. Thus, stories do have a very practical application in the real world and real emotions and real cognitive dissonance occurs when we have to admit that the story we were telling ourselves was wrong.

For the corona event, there have also been two primary stories at play to explain what has happened. The first of these is the title of this book, the plague story, the second is the flu story. A quick note on the terminology here. I am using plague story to denote 'pandemic'. There are two reasons for this. Firstly, as we will see shortly, the scientific difference between flu and pandemic is not clear and this lack of clarity doesn't reflect the mutually exclusive fashion in which the stories are perceived by the average person. Secondly, our society's reaction to the corona event is in line with the technical elements of the plague story. Therefore, the plague story better captures the connotation of great danger and the associated emotional resonance of what has happened whereas the word *pandemic* is too dry an scientific.

The plague story has become the dominant narrative to such an extent that many people forget there was a brief period back before the lockdowns where the two narratives were in competition. Most western politicians were pushing for a version of the flu story and, in fact, President Trump at one point even tweeted that it was 'just the flu'. We were told the health system could handle the problem and there was no need for China-style lockdowns. That battle in the public discourse lasted about two weeks before western government went into lockdown mode at which point western politicians had officially endorsed the plague story interpretation. The plague story became the dominant narrative with the flu story relegated to the 'conspiracy theorist' role.

Before we get into an analysis of the plague story, let's quickly acknowledge that there is no firm distinction between the plague story (pandemic) and the flu story. The US CDC has a webpage to try and clarify the difference between seasonal flu and pandemic flu[1]. It defines seasonal flu as 'epidemics that occur among people worldwide' but this is almost word-for-word the definition of a pandemic - Wikipedia defines pandemic as 'an epidemic of an infectious disease that has spread...worldwide'. Thus, seasonal flu is a pandemic by definition. The CDC attempts to clarify further by stating that a pandemic must be of a 'new' virus that is very different from currently circulating viruses. This seemingly simple word 'new' is itself ambiguous and we will devote the whole of chapter four to a discussion of it. For now, let's just say that the implicit issue here is that the immune system cannot recognise the virus and this is what makes a 'new' virus more problematic. But how do we know that the immune system will not recognise the virus? Even for sars-cov-2, studies have shown pre-existing immunity among the population even though the virus was said to be 'new'[2].

So, ambiguity reigns. Scientifically speaking, the distinction between the flu story and the plague story is not clear. This lack of clarity and certainty in the science permeates the whole corona event and goes right to the heart of analytical problems with viral disease. What has happened time and again is that the public discourse simply ignored the uncertainty and jumped to conclusions. More specifically, we jumped to the plague story conclusion. A great example of this can be seen from an appearance by Australia's Chief Medical Officer on breakfast television way back on January 22nd. The entire transcript is short and worth a read[3]. It contains both the flu story and the plague story interwoven. On the one hand, we hear of a 'deadly new virus'. On the other hand, we hear that it causes pneumonia and flu-like symptoms. The Chief Medical Officer warns that it probably jumped across from animals in Wuhan (more on that in chapter 4) but also says that coronaviruses are common in humans and cause colds. The host of the program asks how to tell whether the virus is different from flu and then states 'this is something like out of the movies, isn't it, these sort of viruses that spread everywhere.' This last point is crucially revealing. The movies (alongside television) are our primary storytelling device in the modern world and, as we will see shortly, they are responsible for defining the modern plague story. That a television host would refer to them directly is no coincidence. In his mind and the mind of the viewers, the plague story was already taking shape and was being used to interpret the corona event right from the start.

Let's now look in detail at the structure of that story.

The Plague Story

The plague story is quite literally one of the oldest known to man. The Bible contains some 156 references to plague. Plague stories also cut across cultures and are as good as a universal. That is why the corona event could truly be a global story because people all around the world can understand it. A comparative analysis of the differences between such stories across cultures would be a fascinating read. But for our purposes here, I'm just going to take a few well-known plague stories from western culture and tease out the underlying structure. We'll then use that same structure to analyse the corona event.

Let's begin with Daniel Defoe's *Journal of the Plague Year* published in 1722 but referring to the London plague of 1665. Here are the main elements of that story:-

Role in the story	**Journal of the Plague Year**
The forewarning or pretense of trouble	Rumours of plague in Holland
The purported origin of the disease	Italy, The Levant, Cyprus, Turkey (nobody really knew)
The disease arrives nearby	Long Acre

Ignoring the potential risk	The rumours spread but are not taken too seriously. People went about their lives
Numbers start to go up	Bills of mortality from each parish show increased deaths some of which are put down to plague. This was a hot topic of conversation among the public
Authorities take some measures but downplay the overall threat	Shutting down of public performances, various other small measures
Some people flee	A lot of people flee. Mostly the rich. Defoe can't decide whether to get out or stay to defend his business. His brother leaves
Predictions of complete ruin	Defoe goes into some detail about astrologers, shamans and priests telling the public the end is nigh
Distrust of government/statistics	Rumours that the bills of mortality were being doctored and the number of deaths miscounted
The government finally takes stronger measures	Officials to visit houses to inspect the sick, watchmen put on duty, various other measures announced
Sick people quarantined	In their homes
The disease spreads and people become desperate	Many stories of people escaping their houses, bribing guards, threatening them with violence etc.

Government ups the ante in response	It's not clear whether London on the whole was closed, but some boroughs in London had closed their gates to travel and it seems the residents of each borough were policing their own borders
People breaking the rules are denounced	Defoe refers to this offhand although he has compassion for those trying to flee
Everyday life is changed	Defoe tells the story of him visiting one of the mass burial pits out of curiosity. Various other stories of people dying *en masse* and the effects on civilians
People endure passively	Not in this case. It seems people tried anything and authorities were mostly powerless to stop them
Medical/Expert response	Quacks selling fake cures
The Plague ends	The plague retreats and people are jubilant. Even though the risk is not completely gone, nobody cares anymore and parties and celebration ensue. The people who had fled now return to London.

This is probably very close to the most basic story of pandemic throughout history and across cultures. We will see how the other stories start with this template and add elements. Let's move to the next which is Albert Camus' *The Plague* published in 1947. This story is close enough to modern times to be a kind of bridge between the old plague story and the modern one but still belonging more to the old.

Role in the story	The Plague
The forewarning or pretense of trouble	Rats dying in the street
The purported origin of the disease	Not really discussed except in the surprise that bubonic plague should appear in the modern world
The disease arrives nearby	The porter in Dr Rieux's apartment block dies. Several other people die with similar symptoms
Ignoring the potential risk	Rumours of an epidemic spread among the people. Dr Rieux plays them down as it's too early to know. Life goes on as normal
Numbers start to go up	Hospital beds are full. Death statistics start to be compiled by the town clerk. They are increasing
Authorities take some measures but downplay the overall threat	Dr Rieux goes to the authorities but they are wary of panicking the public. Announcements with some basic advice are made
What to call the disease?	**They talk of calling it 'plague' but that is considered a big move that will startle the public. Other ideas are mentioned and eventually no specific disease is named in public at this time**
Some people flee	A criminal in the story sets up a people smuggling business once the town gates are closed

Predictions of complete ruin	Doctor Rieux predicts up to half the town could die. A priest tells the people they are getting what they deserve. Local printing firms start printing prophecies which are eagerly consumed by the public
Distrust of government/statistics	Not that evident. The town is locked down and the disease hits before any real discussion
The government cracks down	Town is closed off by official order (this happens relatively early in this story)
Sick people quarantined	Within the town, sick people are isolated in camps
The sickness grows and people become desperate	People shot trying to escape town. Violence and looting. People smugglers do good business
Government ups the ante in response	A curfew is imposed and martial law declared
People breaking the rules are denounced	The people smuggler is eventually captured
Everyday life is changed	Funerals rushed. Normal life overturned
People endure passively	The feelings of separation and despondency are a big theme
Medical/Expert response	A serum is produced but it doesn't work. Some PPE is brought in for the medics
The Plague ends	The plague retreats and people are jubilant. The town is reopened

There are a few differences between Camus and Defoe that I think are worth highlighting. Whereas Defoe is telling the story from the point of view of a citizen, Camus is telling it from the point of view of a doctor and this gives us a slightly different insight because we see the politics of the plague story. We see that local authorities don't want to startle people and create public panic. This is key in the debate about what to call the disease as everybody knows that calling it *plague* will set off associations of great danger. The doctor wants to call it plague because he wants to err on the side of caution and take extreme measures. The authorities decide against it initially in the hope that some small measures will help. As nobody really knows how bad things will get, this seems prudent. Eventually, they are overruled by the central government who orders the town to be closed off and at that point the public is in no doubt about the severity of the situation.

This ability to close off a town also shows an increased power in the hands of the state. In Defoe's day, the government was so weak that it couldn't really stop the public from trying to escape. The King left London at the first sign of trouble and apparently didn't bother himself at all with what was going on. Neither did the public expect him to do anything. By Camus' time, however, the state was powerful enough to lock down a city and use force to impose curfews and other measures.

In Camus' story, we also see the first strands of modern medicine at play in the development of a serum. However, this serum doesn't prove effective and this theme doesn't play much of a role in the story. Camus presents what I would call a *humanist* version of medicine. The powerlessness of the doctors is foregrounded and specifically their inability to ease suffering and prevent death. The doctor becomes simply a witness to death and suffering and such stories are therefore really about the human condition in a broader sense. The doctor is not a hero in the sense that he can save his patients. This humanist story of medicine has been told a number of times. Another favourite example of mine is the Akira Kurosawa movie *Red Beard*, where Toshiro Mifune plays a doctor who knows that lifestyle, poverty and inequality are the real causes of most disease.

This all changes when Hollywood movies become the vehicle for telling the plague story. The Hollywood story features doctors, virologist and other experts as heroes. This relates directly to the myth of heroic science that is one of the foundational stories of modern western civilisation. This myth has deep ties to infectious disease where Louis Pasteur is a prime example of one such scientific hero. We'll go into more detail about the idea of scientific heroism in later chapters. For now, let's look at a couple of examples of Hollywood plague stories which incorporate the scientist-as-hero trope.

Let's look first at the movie – *Outbreak*. This is not really a plague story but a 'save the world from the plague' story so not all the structural elements are met but it's worth examining as it features a virologist as hero.

Role in the story	**Outbreak**
The forewarning or pretense of trouble	A virus is discovered in the Congo thirty years ago. The US army tries to cover it up by destroying the camp where it is found
The purported origin of the disease	Monkey that is transported from Congo to the US
The disease arrives nearby	People die in Boston. A CDC official investigates
Ignoring the potential risk	A brigadier dismisses the risk of the virus spreading
Numbers start to go up	A number of people in a movie theatre in California are infected
Authorities take some measures but downplay the overall threat	
Some people flee	
Predictions of complete ruin	

Distrust of government/statistics	
The government cracks down	The army quarantines the town in California and imposes martial law
Sick people quarantined	The whole town is quarantined
The sickness grows and people become desperate	
People breaking the rules are denounced	
Government ups the ante in response	The army is planning to bomb the town and kill all the citizens!
Everyday life is changed	
People endure passively	
Medical/Expert response	The virologist comes up with a cure but is arrested by a corrupt army officer who wants the virus as a bio-weapon
The Plague ends	The virologist stops the army from bombing the town, has the corrupt army officer arrested and saves the day with the cure

In this story the public is entirely backgrounded and the main battle is between the virologist and a crooked army officer. This is not a humanist story but an action hero story where the virologist is fighting against corrupt power in the form of the army. The virus itself is a source of power in that it can be used as a weapon. (Coincidentally, or not, this is one of the alternative origin stories of the corona event - the virus escaped from the lab in Wuhan where it had been developed as a bioweapon). Thus, Outbreak is a plague story made to fit into the structure of a Hollywood action hero movie.

Now we move to the 2011 movie where the action hero trope combines fully with a plague story – *Contagion*. Full disclosure, I have not seen the movie. I tried to watch it but turned it off after ten minutes. It has the definite feel of a piece of propaganda and I don't like to be so blatantly manipulated while watching a movie. I have pieced this together from a plot summary of the movie. Let's have a look:

Role	Contagion
The forewarning or pretense of trouble	After a Hong Kong business trip, an American woman travelling back to Minneapolis gets sick. We also see people getting sick in Hong Kong, London and other places.
The purported origin of the disease	Bat via pig
The disease arrives nearby	Protagonist's wife and son die in Minneapolis
Ignoring the potential risk	The protagonist demands to know how his wife died. The doctor says it could be any number of things and they'll never know
Numbers start to go up	We see other deaths not just in the US but around the world
Authorities take some measures but downplay the overall threat	A CDC officer struggles to get resources from Minneapolis authorities
Some people flee	A CDC official advises his wife to leave a city that is about to be quarantined
Predictions of complete ruin	Scientists predict global infection with a 25% mortality rate
Distrust of government/statistics	'Conspiracy theorist' blogger

The government cracks down	Cities quarantined
Sick people quarantined	Entire cities are quarantined
The sickness grows and people become desperate	Looting and violence
People breaking the rules are denounced	The conspiracy theorist blogger is arrested for selling a fake cure
Everyday life is changed	Yes
People endure passively	Sort of. Violence and looting too.
Medical/Expert response	Various experts involved in the story. The WHO and CDC coordinate the response of epidemiologists, virologists etc. A CDC scientist creates the vaccine.
The Plague ends	Based apparently on a single test, a vaccine is shown to 'work' and rolled into mass production by the CDC. (This is no doubt a tip of the hat to the story of Louis Pasteur saving the boy from rabies which was also just a single test)

Contagion follows on from Outbreak in foregrounding the role of the experts as heroes. In fact, it goes a step further and explicitly draws the everyday citizen as not having enough understanding of the science to know what is going on and also introduces us to the conspiracy theorist idea which has become so prominent during the corona event (just a coincidence?). A number of elements in the story are spookily like what has happened with the corona event eg. the bat origin element and, of course, the conspiracy theorist character in the story is also a peddler of a 'fake' cure (hydroxychloroquine anyone?).

The reader should note that I am also just a blogger (and author) and so must be a conspiracy theorist according to this version of the plague story. May I also take this opportunity to announce *Dr Simon's Patented Cough Syrup* which makes corona go away for just $19.95. Buy now!

We can see that Contagion is a true plague story in the structural sense. It incorporates the scientist-as-hero trope and introduces us to the WHO and the CDC as the organisations who would be running the show; the perfect segue into the corona event.

Recall from the discussion above that the Australian television show host explicitly referred to the plague story movies during the interview on January 22. Let's have a quick look at what elements of the plague story were already in place when that interview occurred.

Role	**Corona event**
The forewarning or pretense of trouble	News stories from Wuhan. Ties to an exotic seafood market. Stories of people eating bats. Some deaths already recorded
The purported origin of the disease	Bats (alternatively, pangolins or the viral lab in Wuhan)
The disease arrives nearby	In Australia, the first confirmed 'case' hit the news just two days later. 'Cases' had already been found in Thailand and Japan
Ignoring the potential risk	In the interview, the CMO re-assures the public that everything is fine and Australia has a world class medical system
Numbers start to go up	More 'cases' were identified in the following weeks and months

We can see that the plague story had already taken shape right from the start of the corona event. In the modern plague story as shown in the movies, the WHO and public health bureaucracies are also involved from the beginning and that had already happened in this case too. The virus was 'new' in the sense that it was newly discovered. The question of whether it was new to the human population had not be shown at that point but that was the strong implication from the stories of the seafood market and/or the bat origin hypothesis. As things progressed, more and more elements of the plague story were filled in. I invite the reader to think about the chronological unfolding in their location which should correspond very closely to the elements as listed. Here is the full version of the corona event as plague story.

Role	Corona event
The forewarning or pretense of trouble	News stories from Wuhan. Ties to an exotic seafood market. Stories of people eating bats. Some deaths already recorded.
The purported origin of the disease	Bats (alternatively, pangolins or the viral lab in Wuhan)
The disease arrives nearby	Local infection statistics based on PCR tests run by public health bureaucrats around the world. As a result, you knew exactly when the first 'case' came to your country/city/town.
Ignoring the potential risk	The relative lack of interest in the West about what was going on in China. Very little actual news in January and early-mid February
Numbers start to go up	I think it's fair to say the most detailed numbers ever shown to the public in history (although, detailed does not necessarily mean accurate or informative)

Authorities take some measures but downplay the overall threat	Borders with China and other countries were closed in Feb-early March but politicians seemed to be trying to talk the public out of more extreme measures
Some people flee	This happened in Wuhan most obviously. Also, stories from Italy and other western European countries where workers from Eastern Europe went home before the borders were closed. Stories of rich people going to their holiday homes circulated in many different places including here in Melbourne
Predictions of complete ruin	Neil Ferguson's doomsday model, references to the Spanish flu of 1918
Distrust of government/statistics	Has been ongoing throughout. Depending on which side you're on, the numbers have either been over-inflated or under-reported
The government cracks down	Lockdowns implemented in almost all countries in the West. China locked down Wuhan earlier. Other governments elsewhere took various measures
Sick People quarantined	This varied from country to country but most places saw general quarantine of the sick and the healthy

The sickness grows and people become desperate	Again, depends on where you are. Outside of the hotspots, it seemed nothing much was happening. Whatever sickness there was took place in hospital and was not visible to the general public except through news reports. To the extent that desperation was felt it would have been on a person-by-person basis. There was no general desperation. No violence and looting or social breakdown, even in the hotspots
People breaking the rules are denounced	Social media and normal media have been full of such denunciation since day one
Government ups the ante in response	Again, this will vary from place to place. It's certainly been true here in Melbourne where we have had possibly the longest and hardest lockdown of any city in the world (although not because the public is out of control)
Everyday life is changed	To state the bleeding obvious. Interestingly, we heard stories of mass burial pits in China and Iran and the New York pits where the homeless are buried, which hark back to Defoe
People endure passively	Yes. There was nowhere to flee to in this case

Medical/Expert response	Makeshift hospitals constructed, big deal about PPE gear, stories of intubation gone wrong, stories of overflowing hospitals of varying degrees of veracity, quarantine measures, various cures and treatments suggested, epidemiological models, endless streams of articles in scientific journals, experts appearing in media, blogs, podcasts, public health bureaucrats giving daily briefings, the ongoing story of a search for vaccine etc
The Plague ends	??

Once the plague story became the official interpretation of the corona event, people expected the elements of the story to be fulfilled. Quarantines needed to happen. People breaking the rules needed to be denounced. The experts needed to come to the rescue. All these things became necessary because they are implied by the structure of the story. It is for this reason that we must now have a vaccine because that is a very important part of the modern plague story as seen in both Contagion and Outbreak. Currently, we have a vaccine-shaped hole that must be filled. To leave that hole empty would be like writing a sentence without

If, like me, you've had some very unusual conversations with people over the corona event, it's almost certainly because you disagree over the validity of the plague story. Arguing over details is not going to change minds at this point because what's up for grabs is not this or that opinion but an entire explanatory framework. For those of us that think this is an incorrect application of the plague story, the measures taken seem radically and dangerously authoritarian. However, authoritarian actions are normal during a plague and that is why people who are viewing events through that story don't have a problem with such actions. As politicians have now put their political necks on the line over the plague story, they can be relied on to uphold it. Thus, although Trump tweeted that corona was 'just the flu' earlier in the year, he now explicitly calls it 'the plague' and is pushing hard for a vaccine because, as a canny politician, he understands that the vaccine is required to conclude the story and that this should be done as quickly as possible so that the collateral damage being caused by the public health measures can be stopped.

How are we going to get out of the plague story that is the corona event? Only time will tell. Depending on when the reader is reading this, you may already know the answer. At the time of writing, we still don't know. In any case, this book is not about the end of the corona event but the start. The plague story was being told before the science had conclusively shown that the virus even caused illness. Thus, the question to be answered is why we chose the plague story over the flu story. The answer does not lie in the science but in our cultural, political and psychological makeup. A big part of that makeup is the technocracy which in the case of the corona event means the WHO and the public health bureaucracies in each country. It was they who triggered this whole episode by kicking off the plague story interpretation. In the next chapter, we go right back to the beginning and look at how that happened as we revisit the first couple of weeks of the corona event starting at the end of December 2019.

Chapter 2: Cargo Cult Science

The idea that we live in a scientific society is one of the core myths of the modern west. Of course, it is true that our society is built very largely on the back of the scientific breakthroughs that have mostly taken place in the west. However, we tend to take this a step further and assume that our opinions and our public policy is somehow scientific by default as if everything we did had the mark of scientific approval. This became quite apparent during the corona event with the avalanche of media articles supposedly reporting on the science and the fact that people were referencing those articles in the same way that people once used to quote Bible verses to try and win an argument.

To see what was really going on, there's a useful distinction to be made about what science is. On the one hand, science is a process i.e. the scientific method where you come up with a hypothesis and test it. This process involves other cultural practices such as writing peer reviewed journal articles. On the other hand, science is an established body of knowledge generated by that process. It's the collection of core issues, evidence and explanatory frameworks divided up into disciplines of study such as physics or microbiology. During the corona event, most of the public discourse implied this latter category of science - the established truths category - when, in fact, the scientific process had only just begun. The incongruence didn't seem to occur to most people.

Here was what everybody accepted as a 'new' virus and yet many people treated a single study or finding as if it was established fact.

Science, however, is arguably more than just a process. It is an approach or an attitude or an ethic. One of the best ways I know to explain that ethic is borrowed heavily from the great Richard Feynman. I consider Feynman to be the ideal of a scientist – iconoclastic, disagreeable, stubborn, determined, curious to a fault. The last chapter of his great book *Surely you must be joking, Mr Feynman* is titled *Cargo Cult Science* and, in it, Feynman outlines what it means to have what he calls scientific integrity. Scientific integrity has nothing to do with qualifications and degrees and titles. It has the same relation to institutions that a religious spirit has to do with the church. That is to say, there is no necessary relation. In times when institutions fail, you are more likely to find scientific integrity outside of those institutions just as you were more likely to find the spirit of Christianity outside of the church at various times throughout its history.

What is scientific integrity according to Feynman?

1. The first rule of Science Club is: *you must not fool yourself*. The second rule of Science Club is: You. Must. Not. Fool. Yourself. Although Feynman doesn't say it in so many words, I think of this like a duty of care. Most of us have opinions and we throw them around without a second thought. But, if you're doing science, it means you should have spent some time and energy trying to prove yourself wrong. It means saying something like: 'I believe X is the case. What evidence is available to me to back up my claim? What evidence would I accept to disprove the statement? Have I even looked for that evidence or tried to produce it myself?'
2. Having tried to prove yourself wrong, you should tell other people what you did and let them try and prove you wrong by reproducing your work

3. In telling other people, you should also publish all the things that might be wrong with your idea including ambiguities, experiments that failed, facts that could disprove it or cast doubt on it. You shouldn't just present the facts that back up your conclusion
4. When building on previous research, you must first reproduce that research. You must verify its truth yourself. You should not blindly trust other scientists
5. As a scientist talking to a layman, you should explain to the layman in terms they can understand
6. You must know the limits of your test technique. You must know what your test can say about the world and what it cannot say. Therefore, you will know what you can say about the world and what you cannot say

Other things could be added to this list but I think it provides a nice framework by which to judge whether proper science is taking place and I will refer back to this definition throughout the book.

In this chapter, we are going to walk through the first couple of weeks of the corona event to see how it played out and how it looks when viewed from the perspective of science. An argument could be made that what was happening at the start of the corona event was not *just* science but also a public health response which must include notions of risk. That's true and we will return to the idea of risk in chapter six. For now, we are looking to disambiguate between the actual science that was taking place, the public discourse and the public health response which informed that discourse. Let's begin.

31st December 2019: WHO office in China picks up info about an apparent cluster of 'pneumonia of unknown origin cases' in Wuhan[1]

The WHO and some other organisations run infectious disease surveillance programs where they listen in on media reports in different places for anything that sounds like it could be a problem. While doing this surveillance, the WHO picked up a report by some local media in Wuhan. The information is sketchy. It seems rumours of SARS were spreading on social media but actual tangible medical information is lacking[2]. The WHO asked Chinese authorities for more information on 1st January but, apparently before receiving that information, it issued health alerts that day and the next through its international networks.

Whatever this is, it is not science. From our rules of science listed above, you don't just repeat a claim without verifying it. The WHO apparently propagated a report from a local Wuhan news outlet and social media rumours without even waiting for authorities to confirm it.

Let's review the facts that were being discussed at this time. There was a cluster of people (about thirty) with 'pneumonia of unknown origin'. The questions to be asked are: is it unusual to have about thirty cases of pneumonia in China in the middle of winter in a city of 11 million people? And is it unusual to have cases of pneumonia where you don't know what the cause is?

The answer to both these questions is: no.

It is absolutely not unusual to have lots of pneumonia cases in China and in particular in a big Chinese city where air pollution is very high and many people are lifetime smokers. It is also perfectly normal not to know what the cause of a pneumonia is.

The US CDC says: '...clinicians are not always able to find out which germ caused someone to get sick with pneumonia.'[3]

The American Thoracic Society says: 'Pneumonia can be caused by lots of different types of microbes, and no single one is responsible for as many as 10% of pneumonia cases. For most pneumonia patients, the microbe causing the infection is never identified.'[4]

Depending on who you ask, it seems that we only know the real cause of a pneumonia in about 15% of cases.

So, what does 'pneumonia of unknown origin' even mean? Why would something that seems to be a perfectly normal situation be cause for concern to the Chinese authorities and the WHO? Turns out the phrase is specific to an infectious disease surveillance program that is run in China. China implemented a special reporting system following the

SARS episode in 2002 and the phrase 'pneumonia of unknown origin' is part of that system[5]. The purpose of the system was for doctors to report directly back to Beijing when something seemed wrong. The whole point was to get around the local politics that go on in China and to give Beijing direct access to information on the ground. But the system didn't work. Local bureaucrats still intervened and controlled the flow of information. In the case of the corona event, some whistle-blowers tried to go around local authorities in Wuhan. One doctor in particular became famous because he was arrested by police for messaging colleagues about what was happening. He died just a few weeks later. It was the actions of these whistle-blowers that caused the social media rumours and the media reports and presumably also got the China CDC involved.

So, we can see that neither the phrase 'pneumonia of unknown origin' nor the number of cases on the ground in Wuhan had any particular scientific significance. What happened was that the WHO asked for clarification of a Chinese language media report that it had intercepted as part of its surveillance program. In the meantime, the internal Chinese surveillance program had already been activated and the China CDC was on the ground in Wuhan. Why hadn't the China CDC notified the WHO directly? How many other times had the China CDC investigated such cases without the WHO finding out? How many other occasions have there been in China where local authorities prevented the registration of cases of 'pneumonia of unknown origin'? We will never know but bear in the mind that the whistle-blowers in this case were arrested by local authorities and forced to sign confessions. So, I think it's pretty safe to say that there are lots of such events in China that never see the light of day.

Let's be clear about the situation from a scientific point of view. Around the world every year most cases of pneumonia are of 'unknown' type simply because it's too expensive to test every case. If even rich countries don't test widely, you can imagine what happens in poorer countries. We also know that any cold/flu virus can lead to pneumonia and that there are many cold and flu viruses that we simply don't know about because nobody has bothered to come up with a test for them. Nobody has bothered because it doesn't matter[6]. The treatment you get is not based on the specific virus that causes the disease.

What happened in Wuhan has everything to do with internal Chinese politics. Corruption is endemic in China and the local population has very little trust in the authorities there. This was especially true after the first SARS event where the government was seen to have covered things up. As a result, the average Chinese is already primed to be looking out for respiratory epidemics and assumes the government will try and hide them. The authorities in Wuhan were seen to be covering up what could be the next SARS and rumours started flying based on whistle-blower reports.

So, right from the start we can see that it is not science driving this story but internal Chinese politics. For reasons unknown, the WHO propagated that politics. As a peak scientific body in the world, they were seen to be giving scientific credence to a story before they had any official response from the Chinese authorities. If the Chinese authorities had wanted to handle the situation in Wuhan quietly, the WHO had just made that very difficult.

3rd January 2020: The genome of a 'novel' coronavirus is sequenced. It is taken from a patient in Wuhan who had pneumonia.[7] (This news wasn't officially announced until the 7th)

We have to be very clear what the word 'novel' means here. It simply means 'previously unknown'. It means, no human has identified this virus until now. But we can be even more specific because in this case the definition was a genomic analysis conducted according to rules set by The International Committee on Taxonomy of Viruses (ICTV). Thus, 'novel' means something like:

Calculated by mathematical analysis to be genetically dissimilar enough to known viral genomes to be considered a new type for taxonomic purposes.

Let's put that into perspective. Let's say there was an International Committee for the Taxonomy of Animals. That Committee decides to start using genomic analysis to define the names for animals. Enthusiastic scientists on The Committee put the genome analysis to work and realise there are actually two types of Siberian Tiger. They give them the names: Siberian Tiger 1 and Siberian Tiger 2. That's nice for the scientists but if we want to find out whether species 1 is more dangerous to humans than species 2, we can only prove that by studying the behaviour of members of the group Siberian Tiger 1 and Siberian Tiger 2. The genome analysis cannot tell us that. It can only help us to identify Tiger 1 and Tiger 2.

Same with viruses. The fact that a 'novel' virus has been identified by genome analysis doesn't tell us anything about how dangerous it is. Of course, the virus has been implicated in some pneumonia cases but that's what respiratory viruses do. It's not surprising. If Siberian Tiger 1 attacked somebody while Siberian Tiger 2 didn't, that doesn't prove anything about whether the species Siberian Tiger 1 is intrinsically more dangerous than Siberian Tiger 2. You don't extrapolate from an arbitrary sample. You run proper scientific experiments to prove that theory.

This method of classifying viruses by genetic information alone was introduced by the ICTV in 2012. It is controversial and many virologists have objected to the new system. For our discussion, it's enough to know that the ICTV uses familiar terms we all know from high school biology class[8]. At this point in our story, it was hypothesised that the virus was different enough to be called 'new'. Later, on February 11, the ICTV would officially declare it to be a strain of the SARS-COV species of coronavirus giving the following taxonomy[9]:

Family: coronavidae

Genus: betacoronavirus

Sub Genus: sarbecovirus

Species: SARS-COV

Strain: 1, 2

Where strain 1 relates to the SARS event from 2002 and strain 2 the corona event.

Because the 'new' virus was apparently 87.99% (or 96% depending on the method used) similar to a known bat virus there was a further hypothesis constructed that the virus had somehow jumped across from bats. No attempts were made to prove this hypothesis and, in fact, it is not clear how it is even possible to begin to (empirically) prove it. Naturally, it was this story that made it into the media and has become part of the myth of corona. Scientists have spent most of this year explaining that sars-cov-2 almost certainly didn't come from bats directly but it was too late. Because this claim is an important part of the plague story that is the corona event (the purported origin of the disease), we will look at it in detail in chapter four.

Let's be very clear about this from a scientific point of view. All that has happened by this stage in the corona event is that some scientists in China think they have found a virus that is different enough from known viruses to be taxonomically new. At this point there had been no official publication, no official scientific paper outlining their methods, no peer review to check those methods, no other scientists verifying the work, no official ruling from the ICTV that the virus is taxonomically new, no confirmation from the WHO that the disease was new, no proof and not even the attempt at proving that the virus in question ***causes*** illness or what specific sort of illness it causes, no empirical studies at all that this virus caused a unique or particularly deadly kind of illness.

Two days later, the WHO would issue a statement saying basically the same thing I have just said.

5th January 2020: the WHO issues a statement[10]

'The symptoms reported among the patients are common to several respiratory diseases, and pneumonia is common in the winter season; however, the occurrence of 44 cases of pneumonia requiring hospitalization clustered in space and time should be handled prudently.'

It would have been nice if things were handled prudently. But prudence was about to get thrown out the window because...

1st-16th January 2020: the genome of the 'novel' virus is shared with researchers worldwide and PCR tests are created

The Chinese researchers had found a genome and mathematical analysis told them it was 'new'. On the basis of that result, they uploaded that genome to at least two international repositories. One of those repositories is called GISAID. GISAID's mission in its own words is:

'...overcoming disincentive hurdles and restrictions, which discourage or prevented [*sic*] sharing of virological data prior to formal publication.'[11]

'Prior to formal publication' means prior to even the first step in the peer review process so it seems the people who started GISAID were explicitly trying to bypass peer review. Sometimes restrictions and hurdles are there for a good reason. Sometimes it is good not share information when you haven't spent the time to do basic checks of your own work or had others verify it. Like Chesterton's Gate, if you don't know the reason a scientific restriction is there, maybe you shouldn't get rid of it. But getting rid of hurdles is apparently the whole point of GISAID.

We saw earlier that Feynman's number one principle is: don't fool yourself. In biological sciences all kinds of gates and hurdles and restrictions have been put in place over decades for the primary purpose of ensuring that the scientist didn't fool themselves. Among these are peer review, control tests, blind tests, placebo tests etc. These restrictions are built into the process because they lead to good science. Good science is cautious and careful. You share with others in order for them to check your work. In modern virology with its genetic analysis, however, there isn't much to check. The maths is all handled by algorithms on a computer and thus if the algorithm says you have a new virus then that is what you have. It wasn't until the 11 February that the ICTV officially agreed the virus was 'new' but many countries had already been testing for the virus for several weeks at that point. This was because the genome data had been uploaded and virologists and other scientists around the world could now use it to do things like create PCR tests. That's exactly what they did. The German virologist, Christian Drosten, was the first outside China to create such a test which he submitted to the WHO[12]. The Chinese authorities were already using their own test kits early in January[13]. On the basis of the genomic information and the PCR test, authorities in Thailand and then Japan were able to test for and find 'infections' on 13th January and 15th January respectively. The Chinese government locked down Wuhan on 23rd January based on the results of the PCR tests. Other countries started testing and found 'infections'. The rest, as they say, is history.

Health systems around the world started testing for 'infections' before the scientific process had got underway. There had been no formal publication showing the virus was the cause of the pneumonia in Wuhan. All they had at that point was correlation based off a very small sample. No peer review had been done and no experimental results had been published. Neither the WHO nor the ICTV had given official recognition to either the virus or the supposed disease. Recall from the first chapter that, here in Australia, the Chief Medical Officer was already on television talking about a possible pandemic before any scientific review had happened.

Remember the first rule of Science Club: don't fool yourself.

If you ramp up testing, you are going to find 'infections' and it's going to look for all the world like you have a problem. As a scientist, you must stop, take a deep breath and try and put things into perspective so you don't fool yourself. But that didn't happen. Public health bureaucrats started to find infections and they panicked. The Chinese government panicked so much they shut down an entire city of 11 million people. Two months later at the end of March, when most countries in the west were going into lockdown, a scientific paper was published in the New England Journal of Medicine[14]. Contained in it is this warning:

'Care should be taken in interpreting the speed of growth in cases in January, given an increase in the availability and use of testing kits as time has progressed.'

In other words, the more you test, the more you will find. This warning about naïve testing has been repeated in different ways during the corona event. As many people seem to struggle to understand it, let's take a moment to review it.

A Brief Interlude: the more you test the more you find

What that warning in the New England Journal of Medicine meant was: if you test more, you will find more cases. This is a general fact about human perception. Ever noticed how if you buy a car, you start seeing the same car everywhere? There are no more of that car than there were before, it's just that you started noticing them. You had inadvertently primed yourself to look for that model of car. You can deliberately prime yourself to look for things and use this as an exercise in training perception. Go for a walk and decide in advance what you will notice. Maybe it's everything red or everything square or all the birds you can hear or all the smells you can smell. Whatever it is you decide to look for, you will find. The same idea holds in science.

The WHO even stated this notion in relation to coronaviruses in general: 'As surveillance improves more coronaviruses are likely to be identified.'[15] The reason many people misunderstand this idea in relation to the science behind the corona event is because they have an incorrect understanding of how much we know about viruses. So, let me repeat what I stated earlier:

We don't know about many of the viruses that cause respiratory illness.

This is literally true. You can check the influenza surveillance program in your country to confirm it. In Australia, we mostly test for influenza but even when we test for other viruses the result mostly comes back negative. That is, if you show up to hospital with advanced flu symptoms, if they even bother to test you, the test will probably come back negative. That is the normal state of affairs. And that's just for the infections that get to hospital. Countless more infections will never get tested because the people who have them are asymptomatic or only mildly ill. We don't know about most of these viruses because we simply haven't had the technology to enable us to find them. Think about it this way. Suppose there is an area of the night sky that nobody has ever looked at before. Maybe there is some religious prohibition about looking at that part of the night sky. We know there will be stars in that part of the night sky and we know that if we started looking we would find stars. If somebody broke the rule and looked and found a star it would be completely obvious and nothing to write home about. Maybe that person would name the star after themselves and we would think they were an egotistical jerk. Maybe they would win an award for finding the star and then everybody else who wants to win an award will start looking and soon we will have found heaps of 'new stars'. The stars were always there, we just never looked for them before.

Let's extend the analogy to include the invention of the telescope. With the telescope you can find new things in the sky. You can run new tests. It is fully to be expected that you are going to find new stuff. This is the exact situation with respiratory viruses. In the last few decades we have built new technology to identify them better so we are going to find more of them. Lots more of them. This has already been happening. The reader may view a graph here which shows that, ironically, the curve of the number of new viruses discovered since the advent of sequencing technology looks exponential. We have literally found millions of 'new' viruses with this new technology. This eagerness and this ability to find new viruses is behind not just the corona event but the other well-known pandemics of the past twenty years. If we are going to keep shutting society down every time we find a new virus, we could be spending a lot of time at home in the next little while.

7th and 9th January 2020: 'Chinese authorities' declare a 'novel' coronavirus

On January 7, 2020, the China CDC released a statement declaring a novel coronavirus had been identified by genome analysis and was linked to the pneumonia cases in Wuhan. I haven't been able to find that document, presumably it is in Chinese. But two days later the WHO acknowledged it and went public with almost the same information.[15]

The crucial information is in the first paragraph:

'*Chinese authorities have made a preliminary determination of a novel (or new) coronavirus, identified in a hospitalized person with pneumonia in Wuhan. Chinese investigators conducted gene sequencing of the virus, using an isolate from one positive patient sample.*'

The language here is cautious. We hear about a 'preliminary' determination based on a single sample. Nevertheless, in the days that followed, the WHO stepped up its activities including a 'meeting on the novel coronavirus outbreak'. So, we went from a 'preliminary determination' to a 'novel coronavirus outbreak' within the space of twenty-four hours based on a single patient sample out of group of about thirty people with pneumonia in a large Chinese city in the middle of winter. All this based on a statement by Chinese 'authorities'. It may be that this is appropriate from a public health point of view; we found a new coronavirus and we tracked it just to be on the safe side. However, the WHO is also a peak scientific body and in the mind of the public it is working on science. When the WHO speaks, other scientists listen. Just two weeks later, on 23rd January 2020, a team of scientists publishing in a European journal on infectious disease referenced the WHO's statement and wrote as follows:

'A novel coronavirus currently termed 2019-nCoV was ***officially announced*** as the ***causative agent*** by Chinese authorities on 7 January.' [emphasis added] [16]

Let's be very critical about the language here. This is a scientific paper in a scientific journal that uses the phrase 'officially announced by Chinese authorities'? Who are the Chinese 'authorities'? Where is their evidence? Where is the scientific paper where these authorities show their work? Those are the questions that a scientist must ask. But the scientists writing this article apparently did not ask that question. And what about the term 'causative agent'. That the supposed virus was the 'causative agent' had not been shown. Nothing had been published to try and show it. These scientists weren't referring to actual research. They weren't referring to a published paper in a scientific journal. They were referring to unknown 'authorities'. So, we had a paper in what is apparently a legitimate scientific journal talking about the *causative agent* without referring to any scientific evidence that purports to prove that claim. That's not good enough. Once upon a time, the 'authorities' said the world was flat. The 'authorities' said the sun revolved around the earth. The 'authorities' said we should burn witches at the stake. History is full of the 'authorities' saying all kinds of things. A scientist must have evidence. That is what it means to do science. If the evidence has not been provided, it's your job is to ask for it, not parrot the edicts of 'authorities'.

The way science works is that, over time, one paper usually becomes the definitive paper that proved a hypothesis. That becomes the paper that everybody refers to when making a claim like such and such a thing was the 'causative agent'. Until that happens, you would reference other papers that purport to prove it and you would say something like Smith et al (2020) claim that such and such a thing was the 'causative agent' however Johnson et al (2020) called the claim into question. The phrase 'officially announced' simply has nothing to do with science. If even trained scientists were propagating the *official announcement* just two weeks later, if the WHO was already treating it as a done deal, is it any wonder the public had assumed the science was settled? In truth, the science had not even begun.

As it happens, the Chinese researchers published their initial findings the very next day - January 24. They finish the paper with the following statement: "Although our study does not fulfil Koch's postulates, our analyses provide evidence implicating 2019-nCoV in the Wuhan outbreak." Implication is not causation. Koch's postulates are there to establish causality and the Chinese researchers were explicitly saying they had not shown that. Nevertheless, the idea had already taken hold even in the scientific community and I have seen other papers refer back to this paper and say that it showed 'causality' which really makes you wonder whether anybody actually read the paper.

If there was sloppy science going on, the WHO was not exactly setting the world on fire either. On February 11, the WHO *officially announced*(!) the new disease: 'covid-19'. They explicitly stated that the disease was named according to the WHO's best practice rules for naming which are as follows.[17]

- That is an infection, syndrome, or disease of humans;
- That has never been recognized before in humans;
- That has potential public health impact; and
- Where no disease name is yet established in common usage

It is clear that principles two and four were not fulfilled in this case. Pneumonia and Influenza Like Illness have been recognised in humans before. They are literally two of the most common diseases that affect humans. We have names for them already. We already know that coronaviruses cause these diseases. In short, we didn't need a new name. No surprise then that months later doctors and clinicians couldn't diagnose covid-19 as a specific disease[18]. It is not a specific disease. Most viral disease isn't. That's why we have the vague name Influenza Like Illness with a grab bag of associated symptoms that try to cover the possible outcomes of a viral disease. Note how crucial this move is to the plague story interpretation. If the WHO had come out and said that sars-cov-2 caused Influenza-Like Illness this would have foregrounded the flu story interpretation. By creating a new disease name the WHO had instead given significant weight to the plague story.

As one final comment on the scientific work going on at the start of the corona event, let's look at the fourth of Feynman's principles listed above: that you must reproduce the work of other scientists. Did other scientists reproduce the work of the Chinese scientists? Or did other scientists go beyond that work to fulfil Koch's postulates and show that it was not just implication but causality at play? This may have happened but I have been unable to find such a paper. On 29th January, researchers in Melbourne, Australia became the first outside of China to recreate the virus from a sample taken from an infected patient (as defined by the PCR test).[19] This meant that it was feasible for them to reproduce and verify the work of the Chinese scientists. Instead, it seems the priority at The Doherty Institute was to create more tests and to get to work on a vaccine. A similar story played out in other countries.

Reproducibility is a fundamental part of science but there are fundamental problems with reproducibility in relation to viral disease. The Chinese researchers above referenced Koch's postulates but these have never been fulfilled in relation to viruses. This uncertainty in determining whether a virus is the actual cause of an illness goes right to the heart of the corona event and we will discuss it at length in the chapter five. For now, it is enough to say that without proper reproducibility criteria, it seems that what has happened in microbiology is that nobody even tries to reproduce other's work. This has almost certainly contributed to what is known as the replication crisis in the bio-medical sciences. Incredibly, most scientists (perhaps 70%) have never once reproduced another's work[20]. In relation to viral disease studies, there seems to be a special set of problems. In a 2010 paper, Lapkin outlines the difficulty in refuting a proposed causal link between a virus and a disease noting that it could take 1-2 years to get a paper published and require a lot of hard work on the part of the researcher[21]. He also notes: "There is also the issue of political sensitivity associated with the discounting of the work of a colleague and of the judgment of a funding agency or an advocacy group seeking solutions to a problem of medical, professional, or personal interest. It is not surprising, therefore, that journals are frequently reluctant to publish such work." What kind of science is this where challenging another's work is made difficult due to 'political sensitivity' and who are these *advocacy groups* and *funding agencies*? Is it really possible that it is the norm in microbiology not to even try to disprove or reproduce other's work? It seems that is really what is going. If so, it's not a recipe for good science.

All of this is part of a larger trend in science since world war two. Gone are the days of the hero scientists. Science become institutionalised and bureaucratised. Scientists now have jobs and careers and pension plans. They are uber-experts that specialise in highly technical sub-sub-domains of the major scientific disciplines. Are they even scientists any more? Perhaps it would be better to call them technicians servicing to the great machine that has become modern science. There is an important distinction to make between a real scientist and a technocrat. A real scientist will be following something like Feyman's principles. A technocrat will be worrying about political implications and funding applications.

We will return for a closer look at the science of viral disease in chapter five. What should be clear from what we have just seen is that the public health response ran well ahead of the science during the corona event. This has, in fact, been that pattern for all the pandemic alerts from the last twenty or so years. For both SARS and swine flu, the suspected virus wasn't identified until several months into the suspected outbreak but this didn't stop the public health response from taking place. This is important to understand because it was the public health response that was telling the plague story in the public discourse. Where scientists were called on to speak to the media, they often through doubt on elements of the story. We will see examples of that in chapter four where we will see that the information provided by scientists was often misconstrued to uphold the plague story interpretation. Having hopefully now made clear the difference between the science and the public health response, in the next chapter we'll explore that public health response in more detail and in particular its obsessive focus on 'infections'.

Chapter 3: An Epidemic of Testing

We have seen that it was the WHO and the public health bureaucracy that were telling the plague story at the start of the corona event. This makes sense as it is part of their remit to warn about possible disease outbreaks. There have been several such warnings over the last couple of decades including SARS-1 and swine flu but neither of those blew up in the same way as the corona event. The questions is: why? Were these really less infectious than sars-cov-2? SARS-1 seemed to spread around the world rapidly and then disappeared as fast as it came. Was this a freak of nature? Not at all. It follows from the case definition of the disease; a definition that is very different from the definition used to define a case of covid-19.

Recall from the last chapter the notion that *the more you test the more you find*. This is true of pandemics as a whole. Most pandemic statistics are estimates because the amount of testing done is very small relative to the assumed overall outbreak and the testing is normally highly selective, focusing on the severe cases of illness. The corona event is the first time we have ever carried out indiscriminate mass testing on whole populations. It is this more than anything that has given the corona event its unique dynamic by allowing a one-eyed obsession with 'infection'. In the terms of this book, the corona event is a plague story based on infection rather than illness. This is not to say there hasn't been illness and death, just that the overwhelming focus of the public discourse has been on infection. Possibly the most poignant example of that was a video of a Spanish television news broadcast which went viral in August[1]. A doctor was being interviewed from a large hospital in Madrid. The reporter asked him what he was seeing on the ground and he said there was nothing much happening in the hospitals; it was the holiday season and things were relaxed. The reporter reminded the doctor of the increasing infection statistics as if to prove that something must indeed be happening. The doctor replied that we must be careful because 'the data can mislead us'. The reporter ignored this call for calm and insisted that there must be a problem reiterating that the infection statistics were going up.

The data can mislead us. That could certainly be the catchphrase for the entire corona event. The 'infection' statistics are just that – data – and data needs to be interpreted correctly. The implications of this focus on infections have not just determined the way in which the corona event has played out. I believe they also reveal some deep aspects of western culture and we will be tracing those out as the book proceeds. For now, let's just think about the practical effects that a reliance on the PCR test has. What most people probably don't realise is that the PCR test only became ubiquitous in the last decade or so. Prior to that, the case definition for pandemics was based on clinical symptoms and contact tracing. Perhaps the easiest way to see that is to compare the case definitions for SARS-1 to swine flu and then the corona.

	SARS event	**Swine Flu**	**Corona event**
Year	2003	2009	2020
Case definition	Hospitalisation with clinical symptoms (fever etc.) AND contact tracing	Single positive PCR test result (but testing limited in the US to hospitalised patients only)	Single positive PCR test result (mass testing of the general public)

Let's trace the implications of these difference by thinking about how you become a 'case'. Back in SARS-1, you needed symptoms that required hospitalisation and contact tracing. That requires two officials to be involved; you need a doctor to confirm the symptoms and then a public health bureaucrat to investigate whether you might have come into contact with an existing case. What did it mean to 'come into contact with an existing case'? This varied from place to place but generally meant you had contact with an individual who was a confirmed case. In Hong Kong, that meant you had come within 0.91 metres of confirmed case, admittedly a very precise measurement and yet almost impossible to prove to any degree of accuracy. Thus, contact tracing is an inherently subjective judgement on the part of a public health official as it's almost impossible to know how close you came to another person. For example, if you were staying on the same floor in a hotel with a confirmed case, what were the chances you shared an elevator or had similar proximity? The US CDC tried to make the contact tracing decision more objective by providing very complicated guidelines but the reality is this is a subjective judgement[2].

By comparison, the CDC guidelines for corona note that a confirmed case is defined very simply as "Meets confirmatory laboratory evidence."[3] In other words, a single positive PCR test result. We can see how much this simplifies the work of defining a case. What happened with the corona event was that all the complicated and time-consuming work of trying to establish contact with an existing case was removed and replaced with the test. Notice also that a doctor is not required either. Where I live in Melbourne, Australia anybody can self-diagnose and ask to be tested. The government has also encouraged as many people as possible to get tested. It is this mass testing which distinguishes the corona event from SARS-1 but also from swine flu. Although PCR testing was available in 2009, it was still relatively limited and the US CDC decided to restrict the testing to hospitalised patients only. With corona, we tested the entire population indiscriminately thus massively expanding the pool of available people to be tested. No surprise then that the asymptomatic rate is high and the number of people who test positive that have acute illness is very low. We would presumably see similar results if we did mass testing for other respiratory viruses.

You would think that should be good news. When I first heard about all the asymptomatic cases, I was relieved. Here was a virus that was weak enough that the majority of people didn't even get sick at all. Instead the message was flipped around and we were told to worry about silent spreaders. This represents the fixation on infection that has characterised the corona event. It also gives an entirely new dynamic to how the plague story will play out. As David Crowe noted in his excellent summary of the SARS-1 event, the case definition for SARS ensured that cases would dry up once authorities started quarantining people[4]. If you could only become a case by having contact with an existing case, it follows that no new cases can be generated if all the existed cases are isolated from society. That's exactly what happened and that is why SARS disappeared so quickly. It was built in to the case definition. With the corona event, the number of cases is guaranteed never to get to zero because there will never be a shortage of people with flu-like illness to put through the testing process. Because of false positives in the test procedure, there will never be zero 'cases'. That is built in to the case definition. This is perfectly well known by the authorities as a press release from Melbourne's Doherty Institute pointed out.[5] Testing of pandemics must be carried out wisely but governments around the world are either not listening to this or are deliberately carrying on with testing even when they know false positives will result.

It is for these reasons that the corona event has been called an epidemic of testing. We have changed the case definition in such a way as to massively expand the number of potential cases and we have included all asymptomatic and mildly symptomatic people in those cases. In and of itself, this wouldn't be a problem but it has been combined with a wilful ignorance to all other factors including severity of illness as well as the economic, psychological and political fallout from extreme measures like lockdown. This is something that requires explanation. Why have the public, the public health bureaucracy and government so readily fixated on the tests? This speaks to something deeper in our society and culture.

It's clear that most members of the public don't understand how the PCR test works, which is not surprising as the PCR is a complicated and intricate piece of technology. Earlier this year in Melbourne there occurred the perfect opportunity for a public discussion about the test when an Australian Rules Football player got a false positive test result - he tested positive one day then negative the next. This was a big deal because it threatened to upset the playing of a football match that weekend. Coaches, officials and football fans (which is to say most of the Victorian public) raised their eyebrows and asked how it could be possible to test positive one day and not the next. The Chief Health Officer was asked to explain and, rather than admit that it was a false positive, made up some story about how the football player must have been at the end of the infection. The public accepted this and life went on. Clearly, the general public was operating on the assumption that the PCR spits out a binary result that is the truth, the whole truth and nothing but the truth so help me God. Of course, this is not true. The PCR test is a calibrated test and is subject to both false positives and false negatives. The whole system of testing involving sample collection and laboratory work adds further possibility of error. Why then didn't the chief public health bureaucrat in Victoria feel able to discuss that with the public? A few months later, I stumbled across a story from Canada where the chief health bureaucrat there found herself in a similar situation and at least told the public that false positives were a thing but that the public could still trust the tests. So, bureaucrats in different countries have had to use judgement about what level of information the public can handle without losing faith in the testing.

I use the word faith here very deliberately because the attitude of people towards the test seems to me quasi-religious. Here in Melbourne at the start of the corona event, there were people queuing around the block to be tested. This was before social distancing and mask wearing were brought in and so we had the strange scene of people, apparently concerned about a super infectious disease, queuing up right next to strangers on the street! I am not a psychologist but it is clear that the attitude toward the test goes well beyond pragmatic understanding. In reality, the PCR is just a piece of technology. It has advantages and disadvantages. Interested readers can see this 2012 paper which outlines those advantages and disadvantages and compares them against the older cell culture methods[6]. During the corona event, the disadvantages have been completely ignored as we quite literally re-arranged our society around the test results.

This blind faith in the tests is also strange in that the method of testing for corona has been different from the way medical tests are normally carried out. Most of us would have had some experience with medical testing which is always mediated through a doctor. That is, you show up with symptoms, the doctor makes a diagnosis and then orders tests to be done to confirm that diagnosis. This is a crucial point. The test *confirms* the diagnosis. It is an aid to the doctor and it is for the doctor to interpret the test result. Let me give an example from my personal experience. I had a skin condition which the doctor diagnosed and ordered a test to confirm that diagnosis. The test came back negative. The doctor was surprised. She was 99% sure that her diagnosis was right and the test must have been in error. We did a re-test and sure enough the result came back positive at which point she prescribed a treatment. That is the normal state of affairs with medical tests. They are one piece of evidence the doctor weighs up when making a diagnosis. If the test result and the clinical symptoms disagree, as they did in my case, the doctor must decide what to do. In any case, the tests are not definitive. If they were, we wouldn't need doctors.

The fact that the public so readily accepted this completely new style of testing and placed their faith in the test results without having any clue how the test works, speaks to a number of foundational stories and myths in our culture including the myth of progress and the myth of science. The naïve attitude to the test on the part of a large section of the public ignores the existence of false positives, the very high percent of asymptomatic 'cases', the complicated nature of the test and all the different kinds of potential error in the test process. That's before you even ask the question whether it is valid to use the PCR as a gold standard test, what kinds of quality control the government was doing on the tests and whether a single test result was a viable criterion for establishing a case. In short, there's 99 problems with the system of testing in place but the public treated the test as an infallible source of truth.

As we have seen, the public health bureaucrats were keen to uphold that opinion. That makes sense on purely political grounds but the reality is that authorities and governments have also been fixated on infections and have relied exclusively on the test to guide public policy. It is this which has morphed the corona event from a simple plague story into what I believe to be the first example in western societies of a high modernist intervention. The test has given rise to a new political dynamic quite apart from its use in health management.

A high modernist intervention

As we saw in chapter 2, with the instant sharing of the sars-cov-2 genome around the world, tests were able to be created even before any science had been published that established a causal link between the virus and the supposed illness. The public health effort ran ahead of the science. This had happened before, most noticeably with SARS-1, but there was no mass testing back then. It wasn't that we couldn't test for infection in the past, it was that such testing was more expensive and time consuming and not able to be scaled up so quickly. With the corona event, public health bureaucrats had the test very early on and were able to put it into action. The result, as we have seen, has been a relentless focus on infections by the public, the media, the public health bureaucracy and politicians. This focus on a single variable at the expense of all other considerations, reminded me of a concept from James C. Scott's book *Seeing Like a State*. It's the idea of legibility.

'Certain forms of knowledge and control require a narrowing of vision. The great advantage of such tunnel vision is that it brings into sharp focus certain limited aspects of an otherwise far more complex and unwieldy reality. This very simplification, in turn, makes the phenomenon at the center of the field of vision more legible and hence more susceptible to careful measurement and calculation.' (Seeing Like a State, p. 11)

Control. Measurement. Calculation. These are the rewards for the narrowing of vision. As we'll see in later chapters, they tie in closely with western science and the society we have built around it. But, as Scott's book shows, they come at a price and the price is all the things you removed from vision. Things like economic, political and psychological side effects. Scott showed example after example of bureaucrats who were removed from the reality on the ground but nevertheless tried to govern or implement schemes through measurements alone irrespective of any other consideration. This is exactly what we have seen with the corona event where the thing being measured is infection. It was the PCR test which narrowed the vision of the public health bureaucrats and simplified things down to where they could be legible enough to 'control'. Control in this case doesn't mean actual control of the reality on the ground. Rather, it is the perception of control that the numbers give. Or perhaps a better way to put it is the perception of certainty. The feeling that you have grasped the 'truth' and that this one truth gives you all the information you need.

In Scott's definition, high modernist ideology borrows the prestige of science to advance utopian social goals. A concept like *prevent a global pandemic* is exactly such a goal. It seems like a good idea. It's hard to argue against. You can't fault the intention. The problem is whether it can be done and what trade-offs and costs are required to achieve it. In practice, science is usually too ambiguous and too complex to enable the levels of focus (simplification) required to pursue such goals. High modernist schemes are almost always carried out through bureaucracy and, as an organisational type, bureaucracy cannot deal with ambiguity and complexity. What happens in practice is that complexity is ignored and simplified metrics are substituted for complex reality. As we will see in the next couple of chapters, the science of microbiology is ambiguous and uncertain. That ambiguity stands in stark contrast to the activities of the public health bureaucracies who have treated the PCR test as if it was gospel and based all their response around it. In this way, their response has been, in Scott's words, 'uncritical, un-sceptical, and thus unscientifically optimistic about the possibilities...'

In the normal course of events, such high modernist schemes don't work for precisely the reason that they are based on oversimplified ideas about the world. However, they can be made to 'work' when combined with authoritarian government and prostrate civil society because they can simply be imposed on society and the costs externalised onto the public. It is for this reason that such schemes have not been tried before in the West because we don't have authoritarian government or prostrate civil society. There are, however, a couple of ways to make a modern western society into an authoritarian state. One is war. Another is plague. Thus, states of emergency have been declared during the corona event that give the government bureaucracy authoritarian powers and render civil society prostrate. It is for this reason that the corona event ticks all the boxes of a proper high modernist intervention. There is the administrative re-ordering and simplification of society seen in lockdowns, compulsory masks, curfews and restricted movement. There is the overconfidence in science to address the problem, part of which is captured in the blind faith placed in the PCR test and the idea that the measures taken are based on science and science alone. There is the use of authoritarian state power seen in the police and the army. And there is a prostrate civil society that cannot resist state power seen in possibly its ultimate form of the public literally being confined to their homes.

The problem with high modernist interventions was always that the side effects and costs were simply ignored by the authorities. This was because the prostrate civil society had no power to fight whatever measures were imposed on it. As the corona event has dragged on, there has been more and more calls from civil society to consider the economic and psychological damage being done. There have also been doctors pointing out that the medical realities have not been considered, that many of the infections are in hospitals and nursing homes and not in the general public, that the virus affects mostly the elderly and immuno-compromised etc. However, these calls have been mostly ignored as the bureaucracy ploughed on with its testing and its infection statistics. Again, this is a common feature of the high modernist intervention.

We can see, therefore, that the mass testing and the case definition used for the corona event have played a huge part in the dynamic of the pandemic. Authoritarian government response is a key part of the plague story. But the lockdowns in western countries quickly morphed into something else. For one thing we were told the measures were temporary but, six months into the corona event, states of emergency persist. A state of emergency is, by definition, short lived. An emergency that goes on for months or years is no longer an emergency. It's a predicament. That is where we are now and the predicament is a high modernist one. Governments and their bureaucracies now fiddle around with restrictions as the 'infection' statistics go up or down. At the time of writing here in Victoria we have a roadmap that relies on certain, quite arbitrary, numbers of infections per day before restrictions can be raised. What exactly is an acceptable number of infections and why is not discussed. It is simply decided by the authorities and that's that. It's this perception of control, the use plans and roadmaps, the use of measurements which give the appearance of *science* that make the corona event an example of high modernist ideology. What's more, because the case definition of covid-19 means we will never get to zero 'cases', there is no clean way to get out of the corona event. No obvious way to end the plague story. Whereas SARS disappeared quickly, corona will not do the same and this means the high modernist intervention has the potential to drag on even over a period of years. In this way, the corona event has now revealed an inherent tension in modern western societies between the technocracy and democracy. This tension has been latent for some time but it is now out in the open for all to see. If governments cannot bring the plague story that is the corona virus to an end quickly, it is quite possible that the tensions themselves will lead to a further crisis especially once the real economic impacts of what has happened hit home. Governments will desperately want to bring the plague story to an end by way of a vaccine. But if that doesn't happen quickly then we will probably see an extended period of conflict between the technocracy and democracy.

***

Before we move on, let's pause and review the ground we have covered so far.

In the first chapter we looked at the structure of the plague story (pandemic). We saw that the scientific distinction between the flu story and plague story is not clear, but in the mind of the general public the two stories are seen to be separate and mutually exclusive.

The plague story became the officially sanctioned explanation of what is going on when western governments went into lockdown. It is driving the public discourse, albeit at a mostly subconscious level. To this day there will be people who refer to corona as 'just the flu', but this position has been relegated to the fringe.

Chapter two reviewed the circumstances that got us into the plague story. We saw that the WHO's early warning system was activated and, through the public health bureaucracy in each country, the plague story was being told right from the start of the corona event. The public health response ran ahead of the science and we even started testing for sars-cov-2 before any scientific publication showing that it was the cause of any illness. For the corona event, the WHO's language and its declaration of a 'new' disease (covid-19) made the plague story interpretation the default interpretation of events.

Finally, in this chapter I hope to have shown why the corona event was different from past pandemic alerts: the PCR test. The international network of laboratories formed as part of the WHO's influenza surveillance program was activated and allowed the rapid ramping up of testing worldwide. This changed the focus from illness to infection both in the public health bureaucracy's response and also among the public and in the media. This focus on infection continues right through to this day. The states of emergency declared at the start of the corona event are ongoing in many places and governments continue to monitor infections and base public policy response on them. This has led us now into a situation where we are in a high modernist intervention, the first one in western societies. The longer this goes on for, the more civil society and democracy must be repressed and this will create a growing tension that will have to find resolution somehow. The cleanest way to resolve the matter would be a vaccine, which is the expected way that a modern plague story ends. Whether the vaccine arrives in time to head off a further crisis caused by the conflict between democracy and technocracy is going to be a critical factor in what the next year or two looks like.

I believe this establishes the main dynamics of the corona event. It is a plague story where the focus has been on infection instead of illness. The willingness of our society to fixate on infection at the expense of everything else points to deep seated ideological issues which we explore later in the book. In the next chapter, I want to provide an overview of the role played by the media who were telling the plague story right from the start. Our analysis will focus on a specific, a key element in that story: the idea that the sars-cov-2 virus was 'novel'.

Chapter 4: There's Nothing Novel Under the Sun

If it was the technocracy (WHO and public health bureaucrats) who kicked off the plague story, it was the media whose job it was to disseminate and embellish it. Of course, the media is in the business of telling stories and has a vested interest in choosing the most salacious one, especially in the last couple of decades where the business model of the mainstream media was almost destroyed by the internet and every last cent of advertising revenue counts. Even once reputable newspapers are little more than clickbait generators these days. Rather than do a general survey of the media's coverage of the corona event, in this chapter I want to focus on a single aspect: the question of whether the sars-cov-2 virus was 'new' as this is a crucial element in the modern plague story.

Recall from earlier in the book that the distinction between a flu story and a plague story is quite tenuous. Even the US CDC struggles to explain the difference and ends up stating that what defines a plague story (pandemic) is that the virus is 'new'[1]. This distinction itself is ambiguous. The influenza virus is not 'new' but it can make a lot of people sick. It does so by changing through what is known as antigenic shift. From your body's point of view, an antigenically shifted virus is 'new' in that your immune system doesn't recognise it. So, what is the difference then between antigenic shift and a genuinely 'new' virus that has, for example, just jumped across from another animal? Actually, at the individual level there's not much difference at all. In both cases your body's immune system doesn't recognise the virus. The difference at the population level is that a larger proportion of people should have some immunity to a virus that has antigenically shifted whereas that immunity won't exist for a 'new' virus and therefore the public health effects are assumed to be more problematic. So, newness is really a proxy for the ability of the immune system to respond. However, even if you had a 'new' virus, it could be possible that the immune system is able to react. In fact, with the sars-cov-2 virus, there is evidence of quite substantial existing cross immunity that presumably comes from exposure to other coronaviruses[2]. The science therefore is not definitive around whether a 'new' virus is a problem. The answer is: it depends. You need to do further research to get a better understanding.

As far as the word 'new' goes, we have to make an important distinction between two meanings:

1. The virus is newly discovered
2. The individual/population has never been exposed to the virus before

When the ICTV declared a novel virus named sars-cov-2, they were referring to the first meaning. The virus was newly discovered and there is a formal process to go through to give it a name and a place in the taxonomy of viruses. But this does not imply meaning 2. You need further evidence to prove that the virus has not infected people before and that people will have no pre-existing immunity. Let's explain with an analogy again from the animal world. If a scientist goes off into the jungle and finds an animal that they think is new, they compile evidence and present it to their scientific peers. The others scientists agree and they give it a name and an official place in the taxonomy of animals. However, nobody would assume that this animal just popped out of nowhere or that it had just evolved last week to be different enough from its cousins to now be 'new'. You would assume it had been around for some time. If you wanted to find out how long it had been around and when it had diverged from related animals, you would probably have to start looking around for skeletal remains and perhaps even the fossil record. Genetic analysis would also a be a tool in such an investigation.

The sars-cov-2 virus was newly discovered in Wuhan but it was still just a hypothesis that the virus had not before infected humans. What evidence would we need to show that it had not infected humans before? Firstly, you need to show that the virus actually is the cause of the illness in question. Then, you could test for existing immunity in the population using serological tests. Note that, at the time of writing (September 2020), there is still significant doubt over the accuracy of the serological tests. If we still don't have an accurate test now, how could we have shown back in the early days of the pandemic that people didn't already have some immunity? Even if we had an accurate test back then, you would need to test a significant fraction of the population to get an understanding of the levels of immunity. This wasn't done, certainly not where I live. If you had shown both of these points though, another useful piece of evidence would be to identify animals on the ground which had an almost identical virus to the one you have just discovered. For example, if you suspected the seafood market in Wuhan as the transmission place, you take samples of animals from that market and test for a virus. If you find a match then that would be a very strong piece of evidence, albeit still mostly circumstantial.

It was this last point that is most relevant to the plague story of the corona event because we heard about the seafood market and we were told that it was likely that the virus had just jumped across from animals either there or elsewhere in Wuhan. Somehow, a specific animal was identified as the carrier: bats. It's not clear how this happened but I suspect it has something to do with the initial genetic analysis which found that sars-cov-2 was about 96% similar to a known virus found in bats, which was the closest *known* virus. Of course, this doesn't prove at all that the virus jumped across from bats in Wuhan, a fact which scientists have been explaining ad nauseum ever since[3]. Nevertheless, the bat story took hold and has now become a part of the myth of corona.

There are countless examples of this and I'm sure the reader has come across plenty. I still know people who refer to corona as 'batflu'. Right from the start of the corona event we've seen people joking about how somebody in China ate bat soup and now the whole world was shut down. The bat story took on a life of its own and became a meme. And if there's one rule of the internet, it's that once something is a meme, it is officially part of the collective subconscious.

To be clear, there is no evidence that the sars-cov-2 virus jumped across from bats in Wuhan. Why did this idea take off? Recall from the structure of the plague story that there is a segment about the 'purported origin of the virus'. In modern plague stories as told in Hollywood movies, the *purported origin of the virus* is almost always an exotic animal. In fact, the movie Contagion used bats for the purported origin element of the story. So, there was an empty slot in the story waiting to be filled and it got filled. The media was involved in filling the slot as we will see shortly. But public health officials also played a role. Recall from chapter one that the then Chief Medical Officer of Australia appeared on television and stated: "But this virus is likely to have come from an animal species where they also exist. We don't know yet which animal species, but in that city of China it's probably mutated and been able to cross over into humans." Notice the used of the word 'probably'. A very common word throughout the corona event alongside 'could' and 'may' and 'might have'. I recall a similar example from a podcast where the special guest virologist was asked to explain the bat story and she prefaced answer by saying *we don't really know* and that the phrase *we don't really know* was going to be true of most of her answers that evening. Everybody laughed and then she proceeded to tell the bat story. The one that she *didn't really know* was true.

So, the bat story was everywhere in the media and it was being promulgated by public health officials and some experts. It, therefore, forms a nice case study about how the media handled the corona event because not only is there no scientific evidence for it but scientists have been explicitly saying it is not true and yet the media has twisted the message to imply that it was. There are countless other article and podcasts and think pieces that could be used to show this but I'm going to choose just two because they are the best exemplars I have found. The first article is from NPR[4]. Note that it was published on April 15, well after the bat story had become part of the official myth of corona. The headline reads 'Where did this coronavirus originate? Virus hunters find genetic clues in bats' and in the third paragraph we see the claim 'Scientific evidence overwhelmingly points to wildlife, and to bats as the most likely origin.'[5]

Note again the qualifier 'most likely'. We also have to be very careful about the word 'origin' here which is, of course, is different from the word 'new'. The origin of a species can go back as far as you like. Scientists now believe that the origin of homo sapiens is in a species called homo antecessor[6]. But homo antecessor hasn't existed for 800,000 years. So, the word 'origin' when used in genetic analysis can mean a very long time. And, in fact, it turns out that the origin of sars-cov-2 in bats - derived from its 96% similarity - is in fact a long time. The NPR article includes a quote from a microbiologist pointing out this exact fact:

'But that 4% difference [between sars-cov-2 and its bat relative] is actually a pretty wide distance in evolutionary time. It could even be decades.'

The microbiologist goes on to claim that there were probably *intermediate hosts* and that the most likely animal from which the virus jumped was actually pangolins. This raises the question why the article is pushing the bat story when the expert is saying otherwise. We'll find out a potential answer to that shortly.

In order to bolster the bat story, the article contains the following statement:

'The 2003 outbreak of SARS was eventually traced to horseshoe bats in a cave in the Yunnan province of China, confirmed by a 2017 paper published in the journal Nature.'[7]

This is a stronger claim. They say it was *confirmed* that the outbreak (not the origin of the virus) was traced to bats at a specific location. That sounds like there is solid evidence. Let's have a look at that 2017 paper.

The headline is 'Bat cave solves mystery of deadly SARS virus'. Again, this gives the impression of hard evidence which the first line of the article builds on by referring to a 'smoking gun'. But then things start to sound less certain:

'Virologists have identified a single population of horseshoe bats that harbours virus strains with all the genetic building blocks of the one that jumped to humans in 2002, killing almost 800 people around the world.'

What exactly is meant by genetic building blocks? Genes, perhaps?

Then we get this phrase: "The killer strain ***could*** easily have arisen from such a bat population..." [Emphasis added]

There's that word again – *could*. In any case, that doesn't sound like a confirmation to me. That sounds like speculation. Yes, it *could have* happened. But where is the evidence that it did happen? The article continues.

'They sequenced the genomes of 15 viral strains from the bats and found that, taken together, the strains contain all the genetic pieces that make up the human version. Although no single bat had the exact strain of SARS coronavirus that is found in humans, the analysis showed that the strains mix often. The human strain ***could have*** emerged from such mixing...' [emphasis added]

So, if you rearranged the genome from fifteen different bat viruses you ***could*** get the original SARS virus. That's not a smoking gun. That's a trial where the judge throws the case out and the lawyers get disbarred for wasting the court's time. Apparently, it took the scientists in question five years scrounging around in bat caves to get that finding so I salute their determination if nothing else.

In one final irony, the article features a quote from another virologist commenting on the research and for the first time we get a wonderful glimpse of real science at work: disagreement.

'But Changchun Tu, a virologist who directs the OIE Reference Laboratory for Rabies in Changchun, China, says the results are only "99%" persuasive. He would like to see scientists demonstrate in the lab that the human SARS strain can jump from bats to another animal, such as a civet. "If this could have been done, the evidence would be perfect," he says.'

In other words, can we please get some real empirical evidence rather than speculation based on genome analysis. Interestingly, Tu's suggestion is a variation on Koch's postulates except in this case you are trying to infect an animal with a virus from another species.

So, the Nature article misrepresented itself. There was no *smoking gun*. The mystery hadn't been *solved*. Nothing had been *confirmed*. Furthermore, the NPR article was happy to go along with all that and use the bat angle for its own purposes. Why were the journalists in these cases so eager to put the bat spin on the story? I have a theory which I stumbled across purely by accident while following up some of the links in the articles.

Towards the end of the NPR article, we are introduced to Peter Daszak, President of the U.S.-based Ecohealth Alliance. Ecohealth Alliance is a non-profit organisation that aims to 'improve planetary health for the public good by uniquely integrating health research and conservation'. The NPR article just happens to contain a link to research that was funded by the Ecohealth Alliance[8]. That research aims to show that the viruses in bats *could* infect humans. It does so by modifying bat viruses in the lab and then seeing if the modified virus can infect human cells. Why is an environmental not-for-profit funding virological research? Apparently, it's to justify their conservation efforts. In Daszak's words:

'We don't need to get rid of bats. We don't need to do anything with bats. We've just got to leave them alone. Let them get on, doing the good they do, flitting around at night and we will not catch their viruses,' Daszak said.'

According to Ecohealth Alliance's website, their 'budget has grown exponentially and, in turn, so too has our staff and our scientific and media outreach"[9]. *Media outreach*? So, it seems that the bat story was at least partly being promoted by an environmental not-for-profit trying to get humans to leave bats and other wildlife alone. Just when you thought the corona event couldn't get any weirder! Apparently, wildlife activists are doing virology these days. A far cry from the hippies of old. In any case, we can see that the science and some of the scientists who appeared in these articles were misrepresented. The media had decided to foreground the bat story and that is what they were going to do no matter what an expert might have said to the contrary. The bat story had already taken hold by that point and I'm sure bats get more clicks than pangolins in the west where most people probably don't know what a pangolin even looks like.

Whether it's bats or pangolins or escaped viruses from labs, all these explanations serve to fill the role of 'purported origin of the disease' in the plague story. That was the larger framework that was at play. The plague story itself had a slot that needed to be filled and journalists were looking for something to fill that slot. To reiterate, the job of journalists is to tell stories and they know, even if only at a subconscious level, where to look to fill in the gaps.

Ironically, the fact that the closest genetic match to sars-cov-2 was a bat virus, is actually evidence against the plague story narrative. Recall that the Chinese researchers ran the genetic identity of sars-cov-2 against known viruses and the closest match was this bat virus which is 96% similar. The microbiologist in the NPR article stated that this 4% probably equates to decades in evolutionary time (other have speculated between 20-50 years). That means, the closest match in the viral database is decades old. Of all the viruses that humans have identified, the nearest one to sars-cov-2 diverged decades ago. This leaves a hole in the story that's two to five decades long. What kind of mutations and adventures did sars-cov-2 have in the meantime? We have already heard about how it jumped from bats to pangolins and possibly through other animals as well. Why don't we know more about that? Has any research been done to try and fill in the gaps? Is such research even possible for fast mutating viruses?

Others have realised this problem with the 4% difference. Here is an example of an attempt to save the bat hypothesis by a story of how the bat virus jumped to miners in China eight years ago and was transported to the viral lab in Wuhan[10]. It just happened to leak out late last year and cause the pandemic. It's a nice story, to be sure. It *could* have happened but, let's face it, *we don't really know* and we probably will never know for sure.

There is another hypothesis that is much simpler and doesn't require bats or pangolins or murky goings-on in viral labs: sars-cov-2 (or some variation of it) was already in circulation among humans and has been for years or even decades before the scientists in Wuhan identified it. According to this hypothesis, all that happened in Wuhan was that the China CDC identified an existing coronavirus while investigating some pneumonia cases. Virologists ran off and made a test for it, public health officials put the test into action and 'infections' started popping up everywhere. It looked new, but really it had been around for a long time. Just another one of the respiratory viruses that we know exist and cause illness but we have not yet identified. There is no evidence I know of that disproves this hypothesis. It seems just as likely as the other explanations. The problem with it, of course, is that it contradicts the plague story and supports the flu story. The plague story implies a 'new' virus. The flu story implies an 'existing' virus. Right from the start, public health officials were already in plague story mode. Nobody was looking for evidence to disprove that story.

I'm not saying that is the correct explanation, I'm saying that it is as good as the others based on the evidence I've seen. In truth, *we don't really know*. And we never will know because these hypotheses are as good as untestable. All we can do is speculate. In the case of the corona event, we speculated in just the right way to uphold the plague story. Every plague story needs a purported origin and exotic animals work to make the story even more exciting. Bats have long had a fascination in western culture as can be seen by the number of horror movies featuring bats (not to mention the Batman franchise) and so they were chosen for the role ahead of the less glamorous pangolin.

The media are in the business of telling stories and with the corona event the story they were telling right from the start was the plague story. It's not hard to imagine why. The media has a financial interest in telling the most dramatic story possible. However, even when there was a genuine attempt to present the science directly, as when experts were interviewed live on television, any ambiguities were simply ignored or glossed over. My favourite example of that was an Australian academic who was asked on television how accurate the PCR tests were. He admitted that *we don't really know* because there is no gold standard test for sars-cov-2 but he expected it was about 70% accurate. The host simply continued on with the program as if that was a perfectly acceptable answer. Bear in mind the country had just gone into lockdown over these test results. You would think that a statement that they were only 70% accurate would have at least caused eyebrows to be raised. But it didn't make a ripple at all. Once again, it seemed to me, that we weren't really listening to the scientists.

To return to my distinction between science as storehouse of knowledge and science as process, the media is mostly interested in the former. They present the scientist as nothing more than a retriever of facts from the great vaults of science. I wonder if anybody has ever tried running a television or radio program where two scientists that disagree with each other are allowed to have a debate. Presumably, the language would be too arcane and the concepts too specialised for a wider audience. As somebody who has attended scientific conferences and listened to and participated in debates, I can say that they are often boring even for the people who understand the domain. Trying to make them interesting to the general public would be very difficult.

This is another change that has occurred in society in the post-war period. As Theodore Roszak pointed out, modern science can no longer engage with the public in the way that science once did. It doesn't capture the imagination or spark any enthusiasm or interest. Most scientists nowadays are technicians and functionaries. They appear on television the same way that a government bureaucrat might appear to report last quarter's results. All of this lends a dull, dreary and inevitable air to science which is no doubt why most people are half asleep when an expert says something like *the tests are only 70% accurate*. In this way the media failed to convey the fact that the corona event was about live science in real time and that when scientists said we *don't really know* they meant that *we don't really know*. Real science is like that, of course. It is ambiguous and uncertain. Different explanatory models are used to best account for a range of phenomena. Disagreement and argument are normal, in fact, necessary to push things forward. In the next chapter, we'll run a critical eye over the science of viral disease to show the science as a live enterprise and hopefully spark some of the interest and ambiguity that has been completely missing from the dreary reporting of the media during the corona event.

Chapter 5: Germ Theory and Its Discontents

Recall from the last chapter the constant use of qualifiers such as 'probably', 'may have', 'might have', 'could have' and the like that have been a feature of the language used during the corona event. These are not accidental. They point to a lack of certainty around what the science can tell us and it turns out that uncertainty goes right to the heart of viral disease and to the question of how to know whether a virus causes disease. Ironically, the PCR test and related technologies have only increased this uncertainty in the last few decades. The corona event could never have happened without the PCR test and the single, simplified metric it gave to public health bureaucracies. But the PCR and other technological advancements have also changed the game in microbiology and we'll have a look at those changes in this chapter so that we can be clear about the huge gap between the science behind corona and the public discourse.

[*Disclaimer: I reiterate at this point that I am not a microbiologist. What follows is my layman's interpretation of the science. I don't believe there is anything controversial here and most points I make are referenced from scientific papers. The goal here is simply to juxtapose the actual science against the public debate. Please use this chapter only as directed and, if pain persists, see your virologist.*]

As we have seen, the corona event has been all about 'infection'. No small irony then that the PCR test itself does not prove an active infection; all it's looking for is genetic code. That code is one that has been identified by a virologist who finds what they think is the virus causing the illness, analyses its genome and comes up with a segment of the genome that they think uniquely identifies just that virus and nothing else. The PCR test, a complicated bit of technology involving all kinds of chemical processes and fluorescent probes, looks for that segment of genome. It is a calibrated test, which means that you have to find the right number of cycles for it to give the most accurate results. Like all biological tests, there will be an error rate and it is up to the technician and others to ensure the error rate is as low as possible. The error rate exists in the test itself (which chemicals are used etc), in the collection of the sample (contamination, invalid sample capture), and in the laboratory processing (technician error, temperature, contamination etc).

There are 99 potential problems with the PCR test and it seems to me that you'd want some very strict quality control measures to ensure that the system as a whole was not producing excessive errors. The WHO does carry out one form of such testing in which it sends various laboratories involved in its influenza surveillance program viral samples and confirms they return the correct results. The reports are available at the WHO's website. The one from 2018 shows a small but not insignificant error rate overall and fairly substantial differences in error rate between different laboratories[1]. In the rush to respond to corona event, we deliberately brushed aside some of these quality control measures. We allowed 'emergency approval' of the test kits, bypassing the usual QA process. We heard stories of whole batches of test kits being invalid. In Melbourne, we had run out of qualified people to take samples so we had non-specialists going door-to-door to test people. We even had self-service test kits where people could sample themselves. In short, we had set up a system that was guaranteed to produce excess error. When the President of Tanzania gave his famous speech about test results coming back positive for various fruits and farm animals, it wasn't surprising.

Setting aside the logistical issues with the system of testing, the main problem from a theoretical point of view is that we were using the PCR test as the 'gold standard'. In Australia, the government considered you to be a confirmed 'case' on the basis of a single positive test. This is a problem because the PCR test does not prove causality. It is not a gold standard test in the sense in which I understood the term. The gold standard test as I understood it was based on Koch's postulates but it seemed that nobody had run that test. In fact, the initial paper published by Chinese scientists, which has seemingly become the definitive reference, explicitly states that Koch's postulates were not fulfilled and uses the word 'implication'[2]. Subsequent papers however referred to 'causation' which is a very different thing. Until you have shown evidence for causality, how could you know that the PCR test was valid at all?

This failure to fulfil Koch's postulates has been invoked mostly by advocates of a little-known theory of disease called *terrain theory*. In our society, the terrain theory is supposedly a fringe theory while the germ theory is accepted and yet, without looking into it further, it seemed to me that modern microbiology had as much support for terrain theory as for germ theory. We will see exactly how much as we progress in this chapter. For now, let's do a very quick summary of the two positions.

Everybody knows germ theory as it is the default in our culture. A pathogenic germ comes from outside the body, gets inside and makes us sick. Louis Pasteur was one of the foremost exponents in his day and he had the idea that a single germ should cause a single illness. Robert Koch came up with his postulates as an attempt to put the germ theory on firm scientific footing[3]. Meanwhile, some version of the terrain theory was actually the default position of most scientists in the 19th century but the version that comes down to us today is mostly attributed to Antoine Bechamp. Leaving aside the specific mechanics of how it might happen, the theory states that illness comes first and then germs are attracted to the illness. That is, the body first becomes weakened and in that weakened state germs are able to gain a foothold. A related idea is that germs are a by-product of normal processes in the body.

Exponents of the terrain theory like to invoke Koch's postulates because those postulates have never worked for viruses and therefore provide evidence against germ theory. Even in Koch's day, it was known that the postulates did not apply across the board. Later, there would be the technical problem that viruses cannot be propagated in pure culture which was a requirement of Koch's third postulate. But more importantly there was the problem of asymptomatic cases and this is where the link to the corona event becomes clearest. As I stated earlier in the book, when I first heard about all the asymptomatic corona 'cases' my first impression was that it was great news. Here's a virus that's so weak that it doesn't even make most people sick. That seemed like a cause for celebration. The media response was the opposite. We heard horror stories about asymptomatic 'carriers' and how this was terrible because it meant that you couldn't know who was spreading the virus from symptoms alone. The strange thing about that is that it is a repetition of the germ theory vs terrain theory debate that was going on back when Pasteur, Koch and Bechamp were discussing the matter. The early opponents to germ theory pointed to asymptomatic cases as evidence against germ theory. The germ theorists pointed out that it was awful because it meant we had invisible carriers of a virus.

Let's return to Koch's postulates.

The germ theorists wanted to be able to prove a causal relation between a virus and an illness. But if you have asymptomatic cases, then there is no fixed causal relation. All you can say is that the virus *might* cause illness. In fact, Koch had to make exactly this modification to his postulates. Where he wanted to say the virus *must* cause illness he could only say it *may* cause illness. This seemingly small alteration in language has been on show everywhere during the corona event. We have heard endlessly about what *could* happen and what *might* happen. Such horror stories go right to the heart of the uncertainty caused by the fact that Koch's postulates cannot be fulfilled. Terrain theorists point to this uncertainty as evidence that they are right. According to them, the difference between the asymptomatic person and the symptomatic one is the terrain: the person's own body. The epidemiological evidence around corona provides some justification for this notion. Statistically, the people who have died were overwhelmingly the elderly and immuno-compromised. There is also a correlation between chronic illness and acute symptoms. The germ theory exponents fought back by highlighting stories of young and healthy people who got sick. But these were rare individual cases many of which were found to be of dubious veracity.

The problem of asymptomatic cases has thus been at the core of the germ theory vs terrain theory debate right from the start and it is still unresolved to this day. There are all kinds of statistics floating around about the asymptomatic rate of sars-cov-2 infections. I've seen everything from 40%-80%. In any case, it's a high number. That the problem of asymptomatic cases should rear its head with the corona event is therefore no surprise. The fact that the public debate has turned what should be good news into cause for alarm is also not a coincidence. It reveals that the germ theory interpretation has been foregrounded at the expense of the terrain theory.

Recall that one of the key elements of high modernist ideology is over-simplified science. A naïve version of germ theory has been implied in most of the public discourse during the corona event. The use of infection as a proxy for disease only makes sense if you assume that infection is going to lead to disease or death in a large number of cases. But that is simply not true with sars-cov-2. The overwhelming majority of cases were either asymptomatic or mild. Thus, the public debate simply ignored the ambiguities in the science. Those ambiguities are have only grown in the last few decades with the advent of the PCR tests and associated technologies. Let's take a look at some of things that microbiologists have been finding.

The Microbiome and the Virome

The naïve version of germ theory, the one that is part of our collective cultural subconscious, is that our body is ourselves and the world is outside of us. The germs 'live' in the world outside and they try to get into our body where they cause trouble. (Note: I use the word 'try' here deliberately. A virus doesn't 'try' to do anything but much of the discourse on viruses is anthropomorphised). This simplified explanation has been in question for many decades. As far back as 1950s, and probably earlier, we knew about chronic infections; viruses that exist in the body for long periods. At that time, just as now, there was an explosion of technological advancement in the identification of viruses. That led, just as now, to all kinds of ambiguous correlations with vaguely defined illness. Huebner wrote in 1957:

'In addition to many opportunities for spurious etiologic associations provided by the simple chance occurrence of numerous ubiquitous and prevalent viruses, some representatives of these agents are demonstrably persistent in the human host for weeks or months . . . and simultaneous multiple viral infections are extremely common.'[4]

In the last twenty or thirty years, we have seen a repeat of what happened back around the 1950s i.e. a huge explosion in viral identification due to technological breakthroughs. We have seen a repeat of the surge in spurious etiological associations once again raising the problem of Koch's postulates. But this time, the technological breakthroughs point to a paradigm shift in what we thought we knew about the human body. The PCR test and other gene-based tools of analysis have opened up a new world but this new world challenges not just the germ theory of disease but our entire conception of our bodies as independent entities. We now know that viruses are literally everywhere in the world. The oceans in particular are a melting pot of viruses but viruses are on land, in the air and all other places. It is said there are possibly 10^{31} viruses in the world[5]. In every human body, there could be 38 trillion viruses[6]. Most people would have heard about the microbiome, in particular in relation to gut health. It turns out each of us also has a virome and the virome appears to be larger than the microbiome. That is, there are more viruses inside us than bacteria[7]. They appear to be in all places on and inside us: our blood, our mouths, our gut, our skin. It also turns out that a significant number of those viruses are exogenous. Even in human blood, researchers have found all kinds of viruses, fungi and bacteria that originated outside the body[8]. All of this is, of course, a huge problem for naive germ theory. We are not self-contained entities just minding our own business and waiting for a nasty virus to come along. We are more like an ecosystem of micro-organisms most of which are in a symbiotic relationship with us:

'Perhaps the most radical change is the realization that most of the microbes that inhabit our body supply crucial ecosystem services that benefit the entire host-microbe system. These services include the production of important resources, bioconversion of nutrients, and protection against pathogenic microbes.' (Young, 2017)[9]

That's right: viruses can *protect us* from other microbes. Scientists are even now starting to research using viruses as a way to combat bacterial infection thus completely turning the germ theory of disease on its ear. What about the viruses that are typically associated with illness? Well, we already know from the large number of asymptomatic cases during the corona event that we can be 'infected' by such viruses without getting sick but the research is only beginning to show how prevalent that is. It's starting to look like asymptomatic infection by potentially disease-causing viruses is the norm. Studies that test asymptomatic people for infection are relatively new but are showing that it is common to be infected by a virus that could make you sick but doesn't.

'Although malaria, most Leptospira spp., influenza, and dengue were identified more frequently among the febrile [feverish] patients, the detection of these same pathogens in the afebrile control group at a nontrivial rate was striking...'[10]

We now know that potentially pathogenic viruses can be inside us without causing illness[11]. We know we can have multiple infections of ostensibly pathogenic viruses at the same time[12]. Another study found that you were more likely to get sick with a single infection than with multiple[13]. Another study found that some viruses require coinfection to cause illness[14]. Yet another study hypothesised that being infected with one virus made you less likely to be infected with another as they are both trying to fill the same niche in the ecosystem that is your body[15]. We are only beginning to scratch the surface on all of this but the findings raise the question: what is it that causes the illness? It can't *just* be the virus. Probably it is something in the terrain too.

All these new findings exacerbate the uncertainty that already existed around Koch's postulates and establishing causality in viral illness. We can't assume there is a one to one relationship between a virus and an illness. This leads to all kinds of computational difficulties if you were to approach the matter in a purely statistical fashion. Furthermore, in order to get reliable statistics, you would need mass testing of the population to try and figure out how many asymptomatic infections there are. But that would be just the start of the problem because now you need to try and figure out which variable or variables differentiate the asymptomatic from the symptomatic. Let's say we have 50% of people infected with sars-cov-2 who are asymptomatic. We want to know what is the difference between them and symptomatic people. It could be the presence of another virus. It could be the absence of another virus! It could be a general state of health or lifestyle matters or geographic factors like air pollution. How do you reduce the number of variables down to a manageable size? That the PCR and other technological advancements have made these problems more pronounced is well known within mainstream microbiology:

'As with traditional culture techniques, nucleic acid amplification technology has the ability to detect microbes that may behave as "true" or frequent pathogens, transient or permanent commensals, opportunists that take advantage of pre-existing pathology or altered host defences. The difficulty in making these distinctions is made more challenging by the extreme sensitivity of the amplification technology.' (Fredricks and Relman, 1996)[16]

Note the language here. That a virus could *take advantage of pre-existing pathology or altered host defences*. That is terrain theory as I understand it. In those cases, it is the state of your body that leads to the illness by opening up an opportunity for the virus to strike. Given that the statistics clearly show that almost all deaths from sars-cov-2 have co-morbidities, it seems that sars-cov-2 falls into this category of an opportunist virus.

It is one of history's ironies that the corona event and the naïve interpretation of the germ theory implied by it should come at exactly the time that microbiology is showing how outdated that naïve germ theory is. If the body is an ecosystem of microorganisms, by default that shifts the focus back towards the terrain theory as an explanatory framework because in an ecosystem perspective you can't worry about simplistic cause and effect; there are too many variables to calculate. You have to fall back to observation of the system as a whole and that is exactly what terrain theory implies. This observation of the system as a whole is exactly what epidemiology does. Epidemiology explicitly does not concern itself with cause and effect. It just looks for patterns by running statistical analyses. (Recall that even the early epidemiological predictions of sars-cov-2 have proven very accurate).

There have been and still are ongoing attempts within microbiology to save the underlying goal of Koch's postulates and put viral disease on a firmer footing. One of the more recent is from Fredericks and Relman who suggested a new set of postulates that explicitly incorporate genetic identification of viruses[16]. Let's apply just the first two to the corona event to see how they fare:-

- **A nucleic acid sequence belonging to a putative pathogen should be present in most cases of an infectious disease.**

Straight off the bat we have a problem. As I pointed out in chapter two, the disease 'covid-19' doesn't have unique symptoms. Thus, it's not clear how to apply the word 'disease' here. You can say the disease is covid-19 but the only way to know that is from the PCR test which leads to circularity. On the other hand, if you say the disease is pneumonia or Influenza Like Illness, then we still have a problem. In Australia, for example, the overall test positive rate last time I checked was about 0.5%. That is certainly not 'most cases' and would therefore fail this criterion. In some hotspots, the rate was above 50%. But is 50% 'most'? Who gets to decide what 'most' means? The problem here is that many different viruses (perhaps around one hundred) lead to influenza-like illness. This many-to-one relationship causes analytical problems right from the start.

- **Fewer, or no, copy numbers of pathogen-associated nucleic acid sequences should occur in hosts or tissues without disease.**

I read this to mean, the number of asymptomatic 'cases' should be less than symptomatic ones. As stated earlier, the asymptomatic rate for sars-cov-2 is said to be somewhere between 40%-80%. So, this seems to be a negative on this criterion too.

Based on what, in my opinion, are the two most important criteria of their list, I would say that sars-cov-2 does not cause covid-19. Am I right? The problem is that Fredericks and Relman say that not all of their criteria need to be fulfilled and that there must be scientific 'concordance' on these matters. But where does that leave us except in a position that we have to trust the experts. The whole point of Koch's postulates was to fix objective criteria by which these things could be discussed. Such criteria are also implied by the idea of reproducibility in science. If I can't reproduce your work because we cannot agree on the interpretation of the results then we can argue endlessly about semantics with no outcome.

There is an idea that seems prevalent in microbiology that all these new technologies are going to open up opportunities for new understanding. I see the exact opposite. There are going to be way too many variables to calculate. It's going to be the three-body problem on steroids. False positives are going to be the norm, not just at the individual level but at the societal level. Hooked up to early warning systems, how can we ever tell the difference between a genuine pandemic and a false alarm if the science cannot give us firm answers? Such questions have now become matters of urgent political importance. Virologists have tools to find new viruses and they are going to keep finding them. Without criteria to establish causality, the public is helpless at the hands of the experts. There can be no point in arguing on the basis of facts because the interpretation of those facts is what is at stake and essentially it comes down to who has the power to enforce their interpretation. With the corona event, we have seen ICTV appoint a working group to *officially announce* a 'new' virus. Their decision is final. Similarly, the WHO officially declared a new disease. They broke their own standards to do that but who can argue against them? They are in control of the global system of public health.

This is not the way that science as we traditionally understand it is supposed to work. It seems that analytical problems in both virology and microbiology are leading us in the direction of having to accept expert opinion. What are those analytical problems?

The best way I know to explain them is by way of a distinction made by Gerald Weinberg in his book *General Systems Thinking*. Weinberg notes that the secret to science's success in physics was the ability to simplify complex systems to the point where computation could be done. There are two paradigms to do this. One is the domain of *organised simplicity,* of which Newtonian planetary mechanics is the best example. The other is the domain of *unorganised complexity* where averages can be used to get representative results, for example with the behaviour of gases in a container. In the middle of those two is *organised complexity* and these are what Weinberg calls *medium number systems*. Organised complexity cannot be simplified to the point where calculation can be done and therefore is not amenable to science in the traditional way in which we understand it.

The naïve germ theory, where the only things that matter are the individual and the virus, can be seen as an attempt to treat viral illness as *organised simplicity*. In theory, infection would simply be a function of a virus finding its way into your body. This notion has been seen in the public debate in the question of transmission of the virus in droplets and the associated question of the effectiveness of masks. Such debates imply that the only thing that matters is keeping the virus out of your body. Of course, we know that asymptomatic infections rates are very high. And we also now see evidence of existing immunity in the community. We also know that pre-existing conditions, co-morbidities, age, obesity play a significant role in predicting illness. Many other factors could also be relevant. Therefore, there are too many variables at play for the organised simplicity approach to be a valid. (Note that treating viral disease as if it was the domain of organised simplicity is precisely the error of high modernist ideology that we have already spoken of. It is an invalid simplification of the science).

What about the idea of *unorganised complexity*? This is about smoothing out error by taking averages over large samples. Well, this is exactly what epidemiology is. Epidemiology doesn't worry about individual factors but takes a population of people and averages out over that population. This can give useful results and, as I have noted several times already, the early epidemiological models about the corona event have proven very accurate. However, unorganised complexity implies stability in the elements under consideration. The behaviour of gas in a container doesn't change or evolve over time (presumably!). Generalisations made about those kinds of systems should hold indefinitely. The same is not true for viruses and viral disease which are open-ended processes of life. Viruses constantly mutate and the body and immune system constantly respond to that mutation. Thus, unorganised complexity also doesn't work for viral illness. The behaviour of a virus in a population now is going to be very different to the behaviour in a year. We are already seeing some evidence of this with the so-called second wave in Europe where the death rate is substantially lower than back in March. This is why epidemiology can't give us certainty in relation to viral disease. All it can say is that this viral disease and this pandemic looks the same as the ones previously studied. This weakness was pointed out right at the start of the corona event by people looking to dismiss the early epidemiological findings on the basis that they could not rule out the risk of something terrible happening.

So, neither approach works. We cannot analyse viral disease as either organised simplicity or unorganised complexity which means we can't simplify it in the way that we traditionally have done in science. Rather, viral disease is an example of organised complexity. It is a medium number system. Models of such systems are fragile and subject to compounding error. They are actually dangerous because they can seem to work for quite some time and then all of sudden they don't work. That is the bad news. The good news is that we are not defenceless. There are ways to deal with medium number systems. In Weinberg's formulation, the way to deal with them is not to put too much faith in models and definitely not in just one model. You take as many different perspectives as you can and you use them not as sources of infallible truth but as heuristics. Heuristics don't give certainty. They aren't guaranteed to 'work'. They must be employed wisely and used judiciously to aim for the best outcome. A systems approach to pandemic would incorporate findings from virology alongside epidemiological evidence and medical evidence. And it would definitely also include the second order effects of any proposed response such as economic damage, psychological side effects, reduced quality of life, reduce civil liberties and all the other collateral damage that comes with a suppression response to a purported pandemic.

This approach requires what we can call wisdom and wisdom implies the full use of all human faculties including compassion and judgement and common sense alongside scientific information. Wisdom is usually accrued through experience and insight and, as such, can't really be taught. It requires what in German is called fingerspitzengefühl. Quasi-tactile, almost intuitive knowledge built up over many years. In many ways, wisdom is the opposite of modern science. The whole point of science, starting with Bacon, was a body of knowledge that was not tied to the person but could be accrued iteratively over time by many different actors contributing a little bit to the storehouse of scientific knowledge. Whether that is actually true of science, it is simply not a valid way to deal with a medium number systems. In the real world, science should be just one input into our decision making and not even necessarily the most important input.

Here in Victoria, Australia, our state premier tried to justify his measures around the corona event by saying he had a 'supercomputer' running the numbers. The implication being that calculations could solve the problem and tell us what to do. But a supercomputer cannot solve your problems in medium number systems. The idea that it can is part of the ethic of high modernist ideology. Hopefully, the reader can now see specifically why that ethic is invalid. It is the application of reductionist science to medium number systems. It is the attempt to simplify systems that cannot be simplified. It is an error that was on display throughout the 20th century and with the corona event we have made exactly that same error again. The fact that we have made that error symbolises something larger about our society. The myth of science and the myth of progress. The idea that scientific understanding alone can somehow govern society. That we can just ask a supercomputer what to do and get the 'correct' answer.

If, in general, the corona event represents an example of the high modernist mistake that was so prevalent in the 20th century, there was a group of thinkers who understand the limitations of the science but who nevertheless argued for lockdown and other strict measures during the corona event. This is the so-called risk approach to pandemic, an approach which takes an explicitly sceptical view of the science. In the next chapter we will examine that approach and see that it also failed in its own way to provide an adequate perspective. That failure will prove important as a segue to the remaining chapters of the book where we zoom back and start to look at some of the larger social and cultural issues that the corona event reveals.

Chapter 6: The Panic Principle

One of my all-time favourite books is Gregory Bateson's *Mind and Nature*. In the first chapter, playfully titled *Every Schoolboy Knows*, Bateson lays out a list of things that he wished were taught in school. One of them is: *science proves nothing*. What this means is that any theory, no matter how well established, can always be overturned by new data which contradicts it. It also means that prediction has limits. Though something worked a thousand times before there's no guarantee it will always work. I think of this quote often alongside Feynman's definition of science I have already mentioned in this book: science is the belief in the ignorance of experts. The scientific spirit is always about questioning and searching and probing. It is about admitting fallibility and welcoming correction. Even the greatest expert cannot have the whole picture. There may be something they missed or it may be that the next result simply overturns everything they thought they knew. In fact, what very often happens with experts is that they stop looking and, in fact, stop being able to see what is right in front of them. All of this can be nicely captured in the single word: scepticism. Science is about scepticism.

Just because we're sceptical doesn't mean we can't trust and rely on science. We can and do rely on scientific knowledge all the time and much of the modern world would be impossible without such knowledge. We can and do rely on everyday physics and chemistry but things get less reliable as we move into the life sciences. I touched on the trouble with biological systems (and by extension with medicine) in the last chapter. It's that they belong to *medium number systems*. Medium number systems feature a large number of variables that can't be simplified. Models of such systems are fragile and complex and small errors can magnify and render the whole thing useless. Worse than useless, in fact, because the models can seem to work for a time and this leads to over-confidence. That over-confidence creates blow-ups when the model eventually fails. The systems thinking approach was a way to avoid such large failures. It is essentially just a call to re-discover the scepticism which is a natural part of science but which our modern 'scientific' society seems to lack. In fact, the corona event represents the opposite. Many people put absolute faith in the experts.

There is a thinker around today who is known for his scepticism and whose work touches on some of these ideas. He is especially relevant to the corona event because he took a strong pro-lockdown, pro-interventionist position: Nassim Taleb. Taleb directed some of his famous scepticism (which normally takes the form of ridicule) towards epidemiologists and in particular John Ionnadis during the early days of the corona event. However, he completely failed to use his scepticism to question the virological arguments. That is a violation of his own principles of risk and has made his position on corona, in my opinion, absurd. For now, let me sketch out what I believe that position to be in the abstract. Let me call it: *the risk approach.* The risk approach does not concern itself with scientific models of medium number systems because it knows they are subject to large errors. Instead, it concerns itself with risk and specifically with exposure. You don't worry about trying to calculate how bad things will be, you worry about how you will be affected if things get bad. If the worst-case scenario happened, how would that impact you and what can you do to mitigate your exposure to that risk.

I like the example of earthquakes in this respect. You know earthquakes are going to happen. They happen all the time. You know some are going to big and some are going to be really big but you have no idea when the really big one is coming. How do you orientate yourself to this situation? You implement building codes which require buildings to be earthquake-proof as much as possible. Maybe you prevent building in areas where the risk is highest. You educate the population on what to do in the event of an earthquake. You structure things so that when an earthquake comes you are prepared. This preparation need not involve prediction and science beyond the most basic observations i.e. that earthquakes happen. It can be purely risk-based.

Now here is a key question: as part of your risk-based preparations, do you put time and money into the science of seismology or geology or whatever other science might be useful to mitigate the risk posed by earthquakes? On the surface, this seems like a prudent investment. Why not spend a little money understanding the science better? Let's say you do this and the seismologists make what seems like great progress and they invent new technologies that seem to be able to identify earthquakes and predict when they are going to happen and what size they will be. Everybody gets excited and corporations are formed to take government money and turn it into early warning systems with advanced and complex testing run through government bureaucrats who specialise in *earthquake management*. As a hardened risk expert, you are duty bound to be sceptical of all this. In fact, you should dismiss it entirely. Models are for suckers. The models will seem to work and everybody will put excessive faith in them. You know that all models of medium number systems are subject to blow-ups. You won't get fooled by randomness. You'll ignore the models and the early warning systems and concentrate on risk and exposure.

The pandemic preparedness programs and influenza surveillance programs that were set up in the last decades were the equivalent of the earthquake early warning system described above. When they sprang into action at the start of the corona event, my expectation was that Taleb and the other risk-based thinkers would be highly sceptical of them. But they weren't. Quite the opposite. What happened with Taleb (and many others) is that he seemingly believed the early warning system without question. He was told a 'new' virus had arrived on the scene. Having taken that at face value, he then appeared to take all the infection statistics and death statistics at face value too. The lack of scepticism and questioning was incredible in a man who has made a name for himself for being the destroyer of intellectual idols.

Part of what has happened with the corona event is that the virologists and public health bureaucrats ran the show while the doctors and epidemiologists were confined to second rung status. Somehow, Taleb exemplified this development perfectly. As I mentioned above, he singled out the epidemiologist, John Ionnadis, for his special brand of ridicule. He made the exact criticism of him described above: epidemiological models are for suckers. Small errors in the model can lead to blow-ups. The models can't guarantee that there won't be a *yuge* and deadly pandemic. In short, you'd have to be a fool to listen to the epidemiologists. What apparently didn't occur to Taleb was that the virologists are also using very complex models and opaque test techniques as we saw in the last chapter. If Taleb is going to be sceptical of the epidemiologists, he should also be sceptical of the virologists. There is plenty to be sceptical about.

So, this raises the question: why wasn't Taleb more sceptical and why were there so many others like him?

Let's return to the distinction between virology and epidemiology. Taleb went after epidemiology but left virology alone. But epidemiology was already telling us from the start that sars-cov-2 was not going to be much worse than a flu. Sure, we should be sceptical of that claim but we should also have been sceptical of the PCR test, the fact that using PCR tests as the gold standard can lead to false alarms, the infection data, the way in which the corona event started, the public panic which was unleashed and the psychological and political ramifications of that. Why would people like Taleb be sceptical in just one way? Just the one way that leads us into a plague story?

The reasoning seems to go like this. We know that the science is questionable, especially early on in a pandemic, so we revert to risk analysis and risk analysis tells us to plan for the worst-case scenario. Because the worst-case scenario is a deadly global pandemic, we must act as if that is what is happening. To put it into the categories of this book: you choose the plague story precisely because it is worse than that the flu story. It's better to err on the side of caution. Taleb had his own story to represent the thinking. He said it was better to mistake a rock for a bear than a bear for a rock.

Well, questioning stories is what this book is about so let's question Taleb's story. We can see that the problem with the story is that it implies there is no downside to mistaking the rock for a bear. Apart from wasting time and energy running away from a rock, there's no damage done. This is clearly not the case with the corona event. Not only has enormous economic, political and psychological damage been done, there were deaths caused by the panic itself most noticeably in nursing homes and in speculative medical treatments such as sedated intubation. So, a more accurate story is, we mistook a rock for a bear and then tripped and broke our leg while running away. Let's think through the ramifications of that story. What if a real bear shows up while you're nursing your broken leg? What if you keep breaking your leg so many times that you can't walk properly anymore? Mistaking rocks for bears and then panicking has consequences in the real world.

That Taleb would come up with story which pretends there are no consequences to a lockdown is no coincidence. When people raised those consequences directly with him, he simply waved them away by saying that people would have stayed home irrespective of whether the government-imposed lockdowns or not. Really? Which people is he talking about? I for one would not have altered my behaviour one bit. On the information available to me, sars-cov-2 is no more dangerous to my health than any other flu virus. Of course, I didn't get a choice. Neither did anybody else. We were all made to run away from the rock. This reveals the political dimension of the corona event and now we see that Taleb was doing exactly what high modernist ideologues do: ignore the consequences. The costs from the corona response have not been borne equally by different members of society. I doubt Mr Taleb has suffered financially from the lockdown. Presumably he makes his income from book sales and investments. The same goes for the media, the politicians and the public health bureaucrats. They are ones making the decisions to put others out of work without facing those consequences themselves. Similarly, how many of the people who are in favour of the lockdown are salary class professionals who have been 'working from home' for the past months? It's clear that the people who have suffered the most are small business owners and wage class employees. The damage done to these people's livelihoods is simply erased by the phrase *better to be safe than sorry*.

So, we can see that Taleb was also following the high modernist pattern except rather than invoke simplified science to justify his position he invoked simplified risk analysis. This went alongside some rampant cherry picking of anecdotal evidence. Here is a story about some child getting sick, here is a story about embolism or brain issues, here is a story about how antibody tests results are coming back very low and we won't get herd immunity. These were neither proper science nor proper risk analysis. Embolism, for example, is also seen in a small number of influenza cases. Should we therefore shut society down for every influenza pandemic? Wouldn't the 'risk-based approach' tell us to do that? There are influenza pandemics every year, maybe we should permanently lock down society in case one gets out of control.

It is for these reasons that Michael Driver parodied Taleb's position with the name *The Panic Principle* (a play on Taleb's beloved Precautionary Principle). The problem with *The Panic Principle* is that it causes damage. In the real world, losing your mind is never a good idea. You would think Taleb should know this from his time trading on Wall Street. The Precautionary Principle, the real one, implies conservatism. It requires not taking radical action that leads to unknown outcomes. Actions like shutting down the global economy for months. Actions like quarantining healthy people and disrupting the lives of hundreds of millions of people. The Precautionary Principle could and should have been invoked against the lockdown. It could and should have been invoked against instituting an early warning system that was guaranteed to throw a false alarm. This is all stuff I would have expected Taleb to be pointing out.

I suspect what happened with Taleb was an example of what Mary Midgley has called *reductionist megalomania*. Taleb reduced the entire problem down to a simple risk calculation based on exponential growth of 'infections' and proceeded to pretend that it was the only thing that mattered. I identified in the last chapter the problem with this approach. In medium number systems, reducing everything down to a single perspective doesn't work. It doesn't matter whether you reduce down to a scientific model or a risk model. Ionnidas didn't have the whole perspective but neither did Taleb. The difference between the two was that Taleb thought he did. Hence the megalomania. No surprise then that it was the risk school that promoted the idea of 'smashing the curve'. A heroic call to action based on a reductionist view of what was going on. Megalomania and faux-heroism often go hand-in-hand.

Our society has not taken a (proper) risk-based approach to the corona event. We have taken a high modernist approach based on a simplified version of the science. That quasi-scientific approach has led to a blow-up. The corona event is an error due to over-confidence in models that we had no right to be confident about. More specifically, it was faith in one model: the virological one to the expense other ones that could have balanced our perspective such as the epidemiological one. Taleb of all people should have seen that failure coming but he was blinded by his own ego and did nothing more than swap a reductionist science approach for a reductionist risk approach. In doing so, he brought to light one of the underlying drivers of high modernism: hubris. We'll look at the problem of hubris and its relationship to heroism later in the book.

The shame of all this is that a risk perspective is an important one. Indeed, a general systems approach considers risk as one crucial tool in the toolbox. It is one lens with which to view the situation. What does the corona event look like when viewed through the risk lens? Risk is about exposure to harm and, in a nice symmetry, the harm from communicable disease comes from exposure to the people or animals carrying the disease. A naïve reading of this suggests that you manage your risk by limiting your exposure or reducing contact with other people. However, as discussed in the last chapter, things are not so simple when it comes to viral disease. Limiting your exposure to others also reduces your exposure to beneficial microorganisms as well as preventing your immune system from generating antibodies to potential pathogens. This exact point was made by two doctors from California in a video that went viral early in the corona event[1]. Thus, reducing your exposure is not necessarily a good idea. Like most things in life: it depends. Should you reduce your exposure to the sun to avoid skin cancer? Maybe. But if you reduce it too much you'll suffer vitamin D deficiency. Should you reduce your exposure to protein, or carbohydrates, or fat? Maybe. But if you go too far you're likely to become malnourished. That's how things work in biology and in nature. There is usually an optimal value between the extremes. Like Goldilocks, we need to find the value that is just right.

Of course, the plague story is predicated on some super virulent new virus that is simultaneously able to infect people and to which our immune system cannot respond. That is the worst-case scenario; the one that both the movies, the media and famous risk analysts love. There was never any evidence that sars-cov-2 fitted into this category but let's, for the sake of the argument, assume that it was and that in that scenario reducing exposure really is the best strategy. There are measures we can take to structure society in such a way that we are prepared. These include reduced movement of people at all levels. Make population centres as self-sufficient as possible so that movement between them is reduced by default. Building codes should ensure every building has appropriate ventilation and buildings are constructed from materials known to reduce disease transmission (wood, copper). Never allow public transport to get overcrowded. Reduce population density in general. Reduce lifestyle disease and chronic illness both of which make sufferers more susceptible to viral illness. Implement other public health measures to improve immune system health among the population including addressing vitamin D deficiencies. Promote healthy and active lifestyles. Re-structure the entire health model to move to preventative medicine rather than the current system of pill popping and symptom mitigation.

These are all measures that make communicative disease less able to spread through society. Note that every single item mentioned is the exact opposite of the direction our society has been headed in over the last few decades. That is no coincidence. We have allowed, even encouraged, our exposure to micro-organisms. Over the past twenty or thirty years we have seen unprecedented movement of people around the world. In any of the major cities you had people from all corners of the globe going through and bringing their microbiome with them. People like Taleb flew all around the world without wearing masks or taking other precautions. They deliberately exposed themselves to 'new' viruses (viruses that their immune system had never seen before) and apparently never gave it a second thought. Now they are worried about a virus coming to them? That doesn't sound like proper risk analysis to. That sounds like panic.

Of course, you might argue that when the corona event started we didn't have time to implement all these structural reforms and we had to react to the situation at hand. Having created a globalised society with free movement of people we have left ourselves vulnerable to the spread of a deadly disease and had to take measures. But, again, this is only valid if you ignore the epidemiological and medical evidence which said from the start that sars-cov-2 was in the range of a severe flu. Neither the risk approach nor the scientific approach is a silver bullet. They are tools in a toolkit and must be wisely applied. Simply dismissing one of them in the way that Taleb dismissed the epidemiological evidence is childish and dumb. It's also incredibly dangerous. In the case of the corona event, we relied exclusively on one tool in the toolkit – the PCR test – to the exclusion of everything else. We committed the grave sin about medium number systems that Gerald Weinberg warned about decades ago and put all our eggs in one basket. In short, we panicked.

Why did we panic? Well there were plenty of people telling us to panic, including Taleb. But the public's willingness to panic also needs some explanation. The message from the authorities early on, at least where I live, was measured and calm. We were told our health system could handle the situation and even the message 'flatten the curve' was about allowing the virus to move through the population at a slow enough rate to not overwhelm hospitals. But that message itself was overwhelmed by a rising tide of hysteria being fed mostly by the media. I would be interested to read a psychological analysis of what fuelled that hysteria. In the next chapter I will touch on just one specific aspect that I believe played an important part in the corona event which is the denial of death in our culture.

Chapter 7: Biophobia and the Denial of Death

When I was seven years old, I asked my parents for a pet cow. They bought it for me. I don't remember if I was surprised at the time but as an adult it still surprises me. Sure, we lived on a farm and there was plenty of room. But, a pet cow? For a seven-year-old? I don't really remember why I wanted a pet cow but I got one. Of course, the problem with seven-year-olds is that they are seven years old. It took me all of two days to get completely bored with the chores of feeding and tending to the cow. My parents were none too pleased and told me that if I didn't take care of the cow they would get rid of it. They weren't lying. The following year we had the cow put down and butchered. We got about six months' worth of dinner out of it.

The act of eating my pet cow didn't strike me as particularly odd at the time. We also had chickens on the farm which we had eaten. One of my earliest childhood memories is watching a chicken that had just had its head chopped off run and jump over a fence that was about twenty metres away. How it knew where the fence was is a philosophical problem that still troubles me to this day. In any case, seeing animals killed and then eating them was just part of life on the farm growing up. I had been rabbit shooting. I had eaten freshly killed kangaroo. It was all perfectly normal.

I've always been something of a troll, especially when I was younger, and I've always had a fascination with how people react to stories that challenge something at the subconscious level. Every now and then I like to pull out my pet cow story and other gruesome farm tales to see how people respond. I've noticed these stories always seem to get a rise out of people who were born and raised in the city. There's another story I have that usually gets city people out of joint. Actually, this one is a thought experiment. I call it: *The Meat Eater's Licence*. The idea is simple: in order to be able to purchase meat, you first must get yourself a meat eater's licence. How do you do that? Easy. You have to kill and butcher one animal with your own hands. You'll show up at the meat eater's licence facility and will be shown what to do and how to do it as painlessly as possible. It can be a rabbit, a chicken or whatever. We'll probably have to steer clear of larger animals in the interests of not violating RSPCA regulations. If you decide on the chicken, you'll be given a hand axe and will cut the chicken's head off. Once it has finished running around like the proverbial, you'll do what my parents made me do as a kid and sit there and pluck its feathers and then you gut it. Job done. Now you have your meat eater's licence and are free to buy as much meat as you like for the rest of your life.

When I started to run this idea past people just for fun, I was surprised by the strength of the reaction it got. Even though it's just a thought experiment and hasn't a snowflake's chance in hell of being implemented, it seemed to touch on something deep. People would loudly insist that they would never do it and that they would rather become vegan (free idea for you vegans out there: badger your local politician to implement a meat eater's licence). One guy reacted especially strongly to the meat eater's licence idea so I threw in the pet cow story too. He was mortified.

'How could you eat a pet'? he asked.

'How can you eat an animal you've never even seen when you yourself admit that you couldn't bring yourself to kill it?' I answered.

My meat eater's licence had accidentally touched on something very important. I've often thought it represents a divide that separates city folk from country folk. But now I believe it has to do with more than just what's for dinner. It has to do with death in general. The question of killing and eating an animal that you knew first-hand is an interesting one. For those who grew up in the country or had backyard chickens or rabbits, it's simply not a big deal. As a child it doesn't cause you any discomfort or emotional issues. It's just part of life. But now that I reflect on it as an adult I would go a little further than that. Killing and eating an animal that you knew makes you more grateful for the animal's sacrifice and somehow for life in general. By contrast, there is something about buying pre-packaged meat that leads to the opposite attitude. The animal is reduced to body only. Not even a whole body, just parts of a body. In the background are the industrial farming practices that every now and then make it to the news with all the horrifying images that come with it. I can sympathise with the vegans for wanting to put a stop to that but I disagree with their solution which is to get rid of all meat eating. My solution would be to put meat eating back into its proper context. An animal had to die. A life was given. Death had to occur so that you might live. You should have to own that and be responsible for it if you want to eat meat. In most hunter gatherer societies, the killing of an animal was accompanied by a ceremony that gave thanks to the animal for its sacrifice. There was also a lot of skill and effort expended to capture the animal. When we killed our backyard chickens, we knew which one we were eating by name. We had memories of feeding it and of its personality. Again, this was never a problem. Quite the opposite. The chicken had had a good life by chicken standards. It lived on a farm in the fresh air, was well fed and got to run around and live its life. The life of a chicken.

By now you might be thinking: what's all this got to do with the corona event?

To revisit the story from earlier. My conversation partner said he would rather go vegan than kill an animal himself. He was, however, perfectly happy to keep eating meat that was killed for him. Another way to frame it is that he was happy to allow death to occur somewhere else where he didn't have to see it but he couldn't bear to see it with his own eyes and definitely not inflict it with his own hands. In my role as amateur historian, I would say this attitude of hiding from or avoiding death became very prominent in our society after world war two. I think there are a lot of factors at play. An obvious one is that the extraordinary amount of death in the preceding decades had caused deep psychological scars. Another is the mass migration of people to large cities where there is simply less death around you and the odds of killing your dinner are about zero. As somebody who grew up on a farm but now lives in the city, I still notice this because a lack of death also equals a lack of life. There is simply more life going on around you out in the bush and as a result you are very likely to come across dead animals in your daily travels.

There are two other factors I want to highlight. They relate more closely to the corona event because they have to do with human death, the medical industry and the public bureaucracy.

Firstly, there was the establishment of national health services and the massive expansion in the medical industry after world war two. In Australia nowadays, 6 out of 7 people who die will die in a nursing home or hospital. Secondly, the increased size of the health bureaucracy led, as it inevitably does, to more and more regulations. In a classic example of regulatory capture, many of these regulations worked in favour of funeral services so that it is now mandatory in some states of Australia for a family to organise funeral services through a licenced company and where it is not mandatory the regulatory burden is simply not worth the effort for grieving relatives to deal with. Both of these factors have led to a massive shift in the way in which we are exposed to the death of relatives and friends.

It is well known that spending time with a dead body (or alternatively, seeing the body cremated) helps the grieving process. In the Irish Catholic tradition, the body would be kept at home for three days during which time family, friends and community members were encouraged to visit to see the corpse and pay their respects. Family members would usually also be involved in the transportation and burial of the body. Nowadays, all that is handled by a funeral company. In most cases the amount of time loved ones will spend with the dead body is very short and the system does not make it easy for longer periods to be organised as hospitals and nursing homes do not want to keep the body around and many people are simply unaware that they are allowed to take the body home. (Whether people would do this even if they knew is another question). Although I am not a religious person, it seems to me that this is one area where the decline of religion has left a large void. We got rid of the time-honoured ceremonies and traditions that aided the grieving process and replaced them with, well, nothing much. In a fashion typical of the modern world there is a now a disorder called *prolonged grief disorder* which is apparently suffered by 15-20% of people who do not grieve properly and suffer long term complications. The cure? Antidepressants. Yet another blatant case of the medical industry selling pills instead of solutions. Surely this is just a symptom of a larger problem in our society: we have forgotten how to grieve. Because we don't know how to grieve, we have never learned how to deal with death. It seems to me this problem has been getting steadily worse in recent decades.

In relation the corona event, an interesting exercise is to find some news reports from the Hong Kong flu in 1968. Bear in mind that the Hong Kong flu was, if the statistics from that time are even comparable to modern statistics, more lethal than covid when you adjust for population size and demographic shift. Despite that, the newspaper reports at the time were almost jovial about it. People had been 'put on their backside' by the illness which had done an 'awkward Grand Tour' of Europe. Any death counts were factual and unemotional. Compare the tone of those articles to the hysteria around the corona event and I think you get a feel for a cultural shift our society has gone through in the past decades.

In the language of this book, the Hong Kong flu was treated by people at the time as a flu story even though it was about as deadly as the corona event. This raises the question of why our society decided to treat the corona event as a plague story. We have already sketched out the main reasons for that; namely, the fact a virus was identified and the alarm sounded early on, the fact that we carried out indiscriminate mass testing of the whole population, the desire of the media and other actors to tell the plague story and the eventual acquiescence of governments in that plague story. It was quite clear, however, that the public also wanted to believe the plague story and I believe at least part of the reason for that is that as a culture we are now in denial of death.

There are many examples of this but the most poignant one in my mind was the absurd discussion around the elderly that was used to justify the lockdown measures. The fact that the discussion centred on the elderly shows, in fact, that there was an awareness of the epidemiological evidence in the general public. People knew that sars-cov-2 was lethal almost exclusively in the older demographic. Again, this is evidence for the flu story because most flu viruses target the aged but instead the message was twisted around into a desire to 'save' the elderly. If you didn't want to go to lockdown or you objected to the other draconian measures, that must mean you didn't want to *save the elderly*. Once again, Nassim Taleb deserves a special mention here because he was a primary culprit in this style of attack and in his case the absurdity is greatly exacerbated because Taleb had previously identified a category of fallacious reasoning he termed, in his usual inelegant style, *paedophrasty*: invoking pathos towards children to try and win an argument. Apparently, he couldn't see that to do the same with the elderly is simply *gerontophrasty* and is no less fallacious for invoking the elderly rather than the young. Gerontophrasty has been everywhere during the corona event. A thought-stopper. A moral high ground from which to beat back all dissent. Who wants to be accused of wanting old people to die? Who's going to fight that battle in public?

The irony of this is that the way we treat the elderly in our culture leaves a lot to be desired. In fact, I would say that our treatment of the elderly is another part of our society's desire to avoid death because we hide the elderly away in aged care facilities and nursing homes. This might be done with good intentions; old people don't want to be a burden on their families. The outcome, however, is to remove ourselves not just from the death but from the years leading up to the death. We no longer have the same first-hand experience of what it looks like for a person to become old and die. What would once have been a normal, everyday part of life is now almost invisible to us. What it looks like to get old is that you rack up a series of chronic illnesses. Health problems that you once got over now stick around. You no longer get over them. You carry them with you. Eventually, something like a flu virus comes along and becomes the straw that breaks the camel's back. The corona death statistics bear this out exactly. In most places, more than 90% of the people who 'died from corona' had at least one co-morbidity. About 50% had four or more co-morbidities. The average age of death was about the average life expectancy. In other words, the people dying from corona were old people at the end of their life. This is perfectly normal. Almost every respiratory virus shows the same pattern. But this is where things get really weird. Because if you pointed out this simple fact in public you were accused of wanting old people to die; a complete non sequitur. The tone of it and the obvious irrationality of it reminded me of the discussion mentioned above about killing your own food. That's when I suspected something was going on at the subconscious level: our denial of death.

As it turns out, the measures taken completely failed to protect the elderly. The majority of corona deaths occurred in nursing homes. In England there were about 10,000 excess deaths of people with dementia in April alone. That's just the people who tested negative to corona. How many others tested positive and died? They died because conditions in the nursing homes deteriorated and because family members were not even allowed to visit. The lockdown which was justified as necessary to protect the elderly failed to do so. I don't believe the lockdown was ever really about protecting the elderly. It was about protecting ourselves. Avoiding death or at least doing what was necessary to avoid blame for it. A cheap moral posturing that hides a deeper problem in our culture: denial of death. But denial of death is denial of life. The measures we have taken for the corona event have been a denial of life. We have locked healthy people in their homes. We have made healthy people wear masks. We have put a stop to life in the interests of avoiding death.

If life and death are two sides of the same coin, is there a trend involving fear of life? The answer is: yes. It's captured in the term biophobia and it links back to my observations of the differences between city and country people. All else being equal, country people are closer to 'nature', even if it is just the nature that exists in landscapes altered by industrial farming practices. The separation from nature of people in the cities has gotten steadily more pronounced in the post war period. To take the example from the city where I live, Melbourne's middle and outer suburbs in the immediate post-war period were more like independent towns and were surrounded by farmland. Over the decades, the farmland got removed and replaced with housing that was mostly on blocks with large backyards in the typical suburban fashion. In the last few decades, as population increased, those yards got subdivided and filled with townhouses, apartments and McMansions. It's now the case that the average suburban block has a tiny yard with barely enough room for a barbecue let alone the backyard cricket matches that were commonplace when I was a kid and any farmland has now been pushed further out and away from daily life. The flight to the suburbs was originally fuelled by a desire to get away from the pollution of the city and towards a cleaner and more 'natural' environment. But the city has caught up to such an extent that there is barely any difference now between living in the inner suburbs and the outer. As a result, city people have been getting progressively removed from 'nature' over the last decades. It's also true, at least in the US, that less city people are visiting nature as seen in the falling per capita visits to national parks[1]. The explanation for this trend is that children prefer to stay home and play computer games or watch television that visit the countryside. Statistics now show that children spend less than thirty minutes in an entire week playing outside, a trend that has been given the depressing name 'protective house arrest'[2]. Is it just a coincidence that we have all been under protective house arrest this year?

Psychologists have started to notice that these lifestyle trends have led to a general fear of nature which has been given the name 'natural environment phobia'. Thus, specific, innate fear of animals such as snakes and spiders has now grown into a generalised fear of being in environments that are not man-made. Children, but also adults, who have this mentality will get anxious just being in 'nature' and will have a desire to leave. There are now even therapy sessions where park rangers will take a group to a national park and help them to work through their fears; like all fears, natural environment phobia is inversely-related to the amount of time spent confronting it. Natural environment phobia is just part of a larger trend in our society – biophobia. It's biophobia that was behind the guy who couldn't bear to see an animal killed. It's behind the people who shriek back at the sight (and smell) of a compost heap or who compulsively scrub their food before eating it.

For most of human history, we were surrounded by nature in such a way that we were a part of it whether we liked it or not. It's only since the start of the industrial revolution that we started to 'subdue' nature and this has been ongoing right up until the present day. The urbanisation of the post war era and then the advent of home entertainment has led to a situation where we are now thoroughly disconnected. This disconnection itself seems to now be a cause of trauma. Not knowing how to reconnect, we double down in a desperate attempt to regain control by avoiding the problem altogether, just like the people who want to leave the national park at the first sign of a wild animal. Just like that guy wanted to avoid seeing his dinner get killed. Just like we try and avoid death. All these themes are related and have come together during the corona event. A wariness of infectious disease is as natural as a wariness of a snake or spider. But, it seems to me, that what has happened in the corona event has gone well beyond what was the situation justifies and in that sense I believe it links back to a larger fear. Biophobia.

Yes, nature can be scary. Yes, nature can be dangerous. That's the reason why nature can also fill us with awe. You can't have one without the other. The feeling of awe and sublimity only comes from the feeling of immense power that cannot be controlled because to control it would nullify it. It's no coincidence in my mind that nature reverence and the feeling of awe which nature can invoke first arose as a unified movement in western culture with the romantics and that the romantic movement began at exactly the same time the industrial revolution and was in large part a critique of it. It's also no coincidence that the hippie movement, the most recent attempt at a critique of bourgeois society and a reconnection with 'nature' invoked the romantics so strongly. I like to call the industrial revolution by the name that Kenneth Clarke gave it: heroic materialism. Our modern society is built on heroic materialism but it has always been accompanied by the shadow of the romanticism reminding us of the power and glory of nature which our increasingly bourgeois lives was repressing and even destroying.

Apart from the deeper philosophical issues at play, our bourgeois lifestyles have been having very obvious health impacts directly related to our desire to avoid microorganisms. Allergies, asthma, autoimmune disease, heart disease, diabetes and even Alzheimer's disease have all been linked to what you might call excessive cleanliness[3]. The removal of children from even the microorganisms of the backyard is now having negative consequences on the development of the immune system. And poor gut health due to imbalances in microorganisms is becoming a chronic issue. So, there are now very pragmatic reasons to address the biophobia that has enveloped our culture. I will return to the larger issues in the final chapter of this book.

When you are excessively fearful you are more likely to exaggerate risk; more likely to panic. That seems to me to be behind the desire to adopt the plague story as the explanatory framework for the corona event. If people are fearful, it's also natural they would look to strong leaders for reassurance. This is what happened during the corona event. There was a call for heroism from the public that coincided with the adoption of the plague story. Where there is a demand, the supply will usually follow. I have already touched on the call to heroism seen in such phrases as 'smash the curve'. Throughout the corona event, heroism arose in a number of different ways which fitted the pattern of high modernist ideology: a prostrate and fearful civil society looking to the heroic experts for help. And the concept of heroism is a deeply ingrained part of the modern plague story as seen in the fact that Hollywood versions of the plague story are basically just action hero movies featuring experts as the saviour. The appearance of heroism and the desire for that heroism during the corona event reveal some important facets of our culture and it is to these we will turn in the next chapter.

Chapter 8: The Desire for Heroism

A high modernist intervention requires authoritarian government and prostrate civil society in order to be attempted. Could it be a coincidence that this is the exact same schematic that exists in much of modern medicine? The doctor is the authority and you, the patient, are prostrate just waiting for them to intervene and solve your condition. Of course, we simply take this for granted and nobody would think to question it. But let's, as a thought experiment, return for a second to the debate between the germ theory of disease and terrain theory.

The germ theory of disease (in its basic form) puts the problem outside of you and in the germ. The solution is the one we all know: some kind of medicine or intervention that targets the germ such as antibiotics. The terrain theory, on the other hand, looks for the problem in you. If you are sick and you go to a terrain theorist for a diagnosis, they may prescribe something to ease the current problem but they will also look at your general condition. Are you not eating correctly? Are you not exercising? Do you drink too much? Smoke too much? Are you overweight? Are you stressed from too much work? Having found such problems, they will tell you to fix them. You'll have to exercise. You'll have to stop eating so much. You'll have to cut back your drinking. All that is going to take effort and willpower on your part and this effort and willpower is not trivial. In fact, lifestyle illnesses are so hard to fix precisely because they usually tie in with emotions, values and habits that have built up over years. People are usually aware what the problem is and their failure to address it can lead to feelings of powerlessness and shame. It is easy to see why you would seek a different solution. The germ theorist offers that different solution. They will have a ready-made fix that doesn't require anything on your part except a trip to the chemist. Of course, sometimes medicine really is the best option, especially for acute illness. However, the modern medical industry now offers a pill even for illnesses such as high blood pressure which are clearly caused by lifestyle and whose obvious solution should be to change that lifestyle rather than take medication. Given the growth of such lifestyle diseases in the last few decades, it's fairly obvious that the pill popping approach is not working. It does, however, make an enormous amount of money for pharmaceutical companies.

Another way to think about the difference between the germ theorist and the terrain theorist is that the terrain theorist gives you the power. They'll tell you that your health is mostly in your hands. If you do the work to get your diet in order and exercise sufficiently, you'll avoid most medical problems, but it's up to you to do what is necessary. With naïve germ theory, the power is in the hands of the doctor and the enormous medical and pharmaceutical industries that stand behind them. You just have to sit back and let them do the research that is necessary to make illness go away. Note that this is the same pattern that we saw play out in modern versions of the plague story as seen in Hollywood movies. The experts are the action heroes who will save the day. The public are just part of the background.

These themes tie in with the larger myth in our culture of heroic science and it is this that I want to explore in this chapter. To be clear, these stories do have a basis in reality. There is no doubt that advancements in science led to a massive reduction in infectious disease, although we should also note that pragmatic measures like clean drinking water, sewerage and general improvements in sanitation also played a major factor and these are not strictly scientific but technical and even cultural breakthroughs. It's not that the myth of heroic science doesn't have some basis in reality, it's that the myth comes to be used as a filter which gets applied to reality unquestioningly. The fact that there have been massive breakthroughs in science does not mean that there always will be. In fact, by the law of diminishing returns, we should expect that scientific breakthroughs in a particular field will slow over time. The fact that our society is built on science does not mean everything we do is by default 'scientific'. But this is how many people think about our society. Like all myths, the myth of heroic science propagates itself in the act of being told. In modern western society, it is Hollywood that does the telling. As we saw in chapter one, the way Hollywood tells the story of science is via an 80s action hero frame where we know in advance that that the hero will win the day and it's just a matter of how. But that is not science. In some sense, it's the opposite of science where you would expect that for every hundred things you try, ninety-nine will fail. In this way, the story that we have been telling ourselves about heroic science is not about real science. It is about heroism.

It's also true that the age of heroic science is over and has been for some time. As an exercise, list in your mind or write down a list of all the scientists you know by name. Unless you happen to be an enthusiast or a scientist yourself, almost every name on the list will have done their main work prior to, or at best shortly after, world war two. If you happen to have more names from recent times, consider whether you know them from their work or from the fact that they appear in the media a lot. The names on most people's list will have done their work before World War Two. That was the age of heroic science. After world war two, science became has become less heroic and more systematised. Scientists now have careers and pension plans. It's also the case that the low hanging fruit in most scientific disciplines has been picked. The average career scientist now burrows away down in a sub-sub-sub discipline where by definition their work is too opaque and specialised to be of general interest. The heroic age of science is over but it continues on as myth.

With this in mind, and reiterating one of the main ideas of this book which is that we use stories to interpret the world, let's turn to some of the ways in which heroism in general played out during the corona event. We will see that the underlying structure of heroic science with scientist-as-hero and civil society as prostrate explains what was going on.

To my mind, one of the strangest things that happened early on during the corona event was the spontaneous adulation heaped on the medical profession. In particular, the scenes in Britain were deeply weird. It became the custom at a certain time of day to go out your front door and join your neighbours in applauding the NHS. Doctors and nurses had apparently become the new football players or rock stars. We were told they were heroes. This reminded me a lot of the kind of hero worship that has been part of germ theory right from the start and nowhere more pronounced than in the person of Louis Pasteur. It was not uncommon for Pasteur to also receive applause and standing ovations when he spoke at various conferences. Whatever his scientific merits, there is no doubt Pasteur sought to heighten that fame and adulation. Antoine Bechamp, his terrain theory rival, did not.

Because of his public profile, Pasteur was favoured among the political class of his time and given various assignments funded by the state. This mostly involved going in to solve problems that farmers were having. For example, issues with the grape harvest or problems with disease among livestock. It seems many of Pasteur's solutions failed and in particular his early attempts at vaccines killed many animals until he accidentally stumbled across the attenuated vaccine method. These failures follow the high modernist pattern perfectly. Here was Pasteur as hero sent in to save the floundering farmers. The prostrate civil society just waiting for the science-based intervention. Of course, there are questions about why the farmers were suddenly having such problems. Was it perhaps because of monoculture farming practices or insufficient genetic diversity in the breeds of cattle? What had changed so that the farmers suddenly needed a hero to come in and save them? Perhaps a scale problem? Too many animals per square kilometre, for example? These questions are a terrain-theorist's questions. They ask about the broader context of the problem. The hero does not necessarily do that. The hero just goes in to save the day.

With the corona event, the public seemed to want this same kind of heroism. This desire for heroism wasn't just limited to the applause for the NHS in Britain. It manifested elsewhere too. Where I live in Melbourne, a mini cult has sprung up around the State premier who has repeatedly taken decisive action including locking down the city on multiple occasions. Nevertheless, I still remember the early days back at the start of March where he, like most political leaders, was accused of dragging his feet. He eventually got the message: the public wanted action. It wanted heroic measures. That's exactly what he has given them since: firm, decisive action. The fact that the decisions made today are completely at odds with the decisions made a month or two ago or that many of measures did not produce any obvious results doesn't seem to matter. Consistency is not required. Just decisiveness.

That the desire for heroism and decisiveness seems to exist independently of results is evidence that it is a myth at work rather than pragmatic or utilitarian concerns. Even though Pasteur's early vaccines killed a great number of animals, this didn't seem to affect his public reputation. Similarly, in modern society all kinds of promises about new technologies and scientific breakthroughs have failed to materialise and this failure doesn't seem to matter. To take just one example: we've been supposed to be going to Mars for decades now. When Elon Musk comes out and promises that it's just about to happen, you would expect some level of scepticism and even cynicism. But nobody bats an eyelid. In fact, articles will be written detailing the plan and how Musk is hard at work to make it happen. Musk is, of course, the prototypical hero. He is filling a role that is created by the myth of heroic science. The myth doesn't actually require results, it just requires that the story be told and re-told. Myths live in the imagination and not in *the real world*.

This desire for medical heroes and government authorities to intervene might sound so obvious to a modern reader that we forget that it's still a relatively new thing that really took off after world war two with the massive expansion of the public bureaucracy and the modern medical system. Prior to that there was a much more self-sufficient ethic among the general public. We saw that in chapter one with the outline of Defoe's *Journal of the Plague Year*. One of the striking differences back then was that people expected nothing from the authorities. The King left London at the first sight of trouble. He moved to Oxford and apparently paid no attention whatsoever to the plague or how it affected his people. This was seemingly not a problem among the public who did not expect that his majesty would lift a finger to help them. They had to help themselves. Where the local authorities intervened, the people would simply try and get around those interventions as best they could. In short, there is no heroism nor any expectation of heroism in Defoe's account. The same was true in Camus. The whole point of his story was that nothing can be done except sit and watch things unfold. This was, indeed, the attitude towards such things for most of human history. Disease was not something that could be avoided. It was a fact of life.

The idea that there is nothing to be done is anathema to our culture. We have become so used to manipulating our environment that the idea that 'nature' could intervene in our lives and there's nothing we can do about it is seen as evidence of some kind of moral failure (you want old people to die?) or at least a severe lack of drive and intelligence. The breakthroughs which led to this attitude, however, are really quite recent; probably only a little more than a hundred years old. We shouldn't underestimate the magnitude of those changes which occurred in society around the time of Pasteur. Prior to that, it simply never occurred to people to try and reduce infectious disease. But the advent of improved sanitation, vaccines and antibiotics did indeed revolutionise society and saw a massive reduction in the deaths from infectious disease. It's not hard to see why a cult of heroism sprung up around the people involved with those breakthroughs. Back in De Foe's day, there was no public health system and nobody who really could help you. The so-called doctors of the time were mostly quacks and you were better off spending your money trying to get supernatural help which at least didn't make you any physically sicker than you already were. In the modern world, we have a sophisticated medical system to come to your aid in the event of illness and that system was built largely on the back of the breakthroughs that came from the likes of Pasteur but also Florence Nightingale who, after all, established the modern profession of nursing and who was, by the way, an exponent of the terrain theory of disease.

There are a couple of points to be made about this. Firstly, the reductions in infectious disease happened quite quickly and the benefits were mostly realised, in Western countries at least, by about the late 1960s. The US Surgeon General in 1967 was so buoyant that he declared it time to close the book on infectious disease and start to address the growing issue with chronic illness[1]. Most people who are alive now (in modern western societies) have lived in a world where infectious disease as it has been known for most of human history simply doesn't exist as a daily fact of life.

The second point is to understand that what we have now is a *system*; a health system. A system is a very different thing from a hero. Back in the day, people sought out the likes of Pasteur for treatment. Such superstar doctors and physicians still exist, but most of us now enjoy the benefits of a system. A system is a collective. It is in some sense the opposite of heroism, which is about an individual. It is certainly the opposite of the Hollywood action-hero heroism where the hero intervenes precisely because the system can't handle the problem. In early the days of the corona event, we were told the lockdown measures were in place to protect this system and prevent it from collapsing under a sudden spike in admissions. This was the 'flatten the curve' mantra. Politicians initially said we could flatten the curve by basic measures that wouldn't require a shutdown of society but there was a revolt against this idea and a demand for tougher and tougher measures. It wasn't enough to just protect the hospital system. We wanted something more. That something more was heroism. This call for heroism was captured best in the mantra to 'smash the curve'. Its negative aspect was to accuse people who didn't want the collateral damage of heroic intervention of wanting old people to die. Don't want heroism? Stand aside please and leave it to the experts.

This example of systems vs heroes is something I have seen in my professional life. Within the cultures of IT where I have worked, there is an active distrust of the hero mentality because what usually happens is that the hero constructs the kind of system where they make themselves indispensable. This is where heroism descends into narcissism and megalomania at the level of the individual. It's the desire for power and prestige. This same psychology can be seen in firemen who start fires in order to come in and save the day by putting them out or in the Munchausen by proxy syndrome. In the world of business, there are good reasons for companies to avoid heroes. The main one is because the hero has too much power. If the hero is the only one who knows how a system works, they can use that to their advantage in salary negotiations. Heroes also make the system inherently unstable because, if something happens to the hero, the system as a whole can grind to a halt. I remember once sitting in a job interview where the candidate was a hero. He was asked the usual cheesy interview question of what he liked about his job and he said something like waking up in the middle of the night and getting the system back up and running. What he might have said was 'I like building systems where I don't have to get up in the middle of the night to get the system back up and running.' He wasn't offered the job. In that company we didn't want heroes. We wanted system builders.

It's probably because of this background that I always get a little suspicious when heroics are concerned. No doubt sometimes in life genuine heroics are required. The rest of the time, it seems to me that heroics are a cover for a poorly designed system. And this is where the cry for heroism with the corona event seemed to me out of place. In some countries, no doubt, the medical system is underfunded and under-resourced. But certainly not where I live in Australia or in places like Germany. Our hospital systems are well designed and well-funded. We should be proud of them. But in the case of corona we apparently didn't trust them. We thought they needed saving by heroes. Was that true? Did our hospital systems really need heroes to come and save the day? In most places it seems that the answer was a firm 'no'. Almost everywhere that makeshift hospitals were constructed, they weren't used. Apart from a few hotspots, most places have not seen hospitals overwhelmed. The models used to justify the construction of those makeshift hospitals were not the epidemiological models based on real data but the models of Neil Ferguson and the like. The doomsday models. According to those models we needed action. According to those models, we needed heroism. In my opinion, we wanted heroism and then we went looking for the models that could justify it. There was never any actual need for heroism. Not in the sense of saving the system.

Nevertheless, politicians could read the public mood and we got a dose of heroism in a never before imagined lockdown of society that was supposed to flatten the curve. But that message quickly morphed into something else. It was no longer about saving the hospital system, it was about eliminating the virus and efforts to get a vaccine. The heroism genie was out of the bottle. All talk of protecting the system was gone. In fact, we were told society itself could no longer function as a system without a vaccine. This is a high modernist grand plan if ever there was one. A prostrate society needing rescuing by heroic experts.

Of course, there are financial interests behind these kinds of schemes and there are no shortage of wannabe heroes to come up with them. But my contention is that a large proportion of the public wanted such a grand plan. There were too many examples of seemingly autonomous action on the part the public that followed the hero script to a tee. One of these was the now ubiquitous shaming and stifling of dissenting voices. If a prostrate civil society is required for the enactment of high modernist plans, one of the more interesting dynamics during the corona event is how civil society became self-prostrating. Of course, the army and the police were used to keep people physically in their homes. But there has also been social pressure exerted on dissenters and this pressure took the form of a strange kind of call for anti-heroism focused particularly on quelling dissent around the lockdown and the wearing of masks. The reader can search the internet for many different examples of the memes that went into circulation. But the common underlying thread in many of them was to juxtapose the hero against you, the lowly everyday citizen.

Here's just one of countless examples where Mr T (the hero) puts you in your place courtesy of a bad bit of photoshop.

Another meme that aimed to quell dissent around staying at home stood out to me. It went along the lines of: "Your grandfather had to fight a war. All you've got to do is stay home on the couch and watch television. Think you can handle that?" Once again, we have the hero (your grandfather at war) and you who are simply asked to do, well, nothing. The irony in this is that many of our grandfathers willingly signed up to go to war precisely because they wanted to leave home and go and have a heroic adventure. But the underlying message in all these examples is the same. What was required of you during the corona event was precisely not to be a hero. You just had to sit back and let the real heroes do the work. Is it a coincidence that this is exactly the form of the germ theory patient just doing what their doctor says? Is it a coincidence that a terrain theorist would say exactly the opposite: of course, you shouldn't stay at home. You should go outside and get fresh air and vitamin D and stay active. You should mix with other people and keep your spirits up.

The fact that this clearing out of opposition from civil society apparently took place quite spontaneously via everyday people on social media is evidence of the underlying myth at work. Just like the people clapping for the NHS in Britain, it seems everyday citizens needed no prompting; they knew the script already. Partly, that script was the plague story element 'People breaking the rules are denounced'. However, there was something more going on and that something more is captured in germ theory, scientist-as-hero and high modernist ideology. As a citizen, you must be prostrate so that the experts can do their work. Individuals in many different places played out this dynamic because they are working from the same ideology; the ideology of high modernism and the myth of heroic science.

Against the backdrop of this kind of high modernist heroism that has dominated during the corona event, I would like to give a different version of heroism, if for no other reason than to provide the reader with an alternative to the Hollywood action movie hero that has become the dominant type of hero in our culture. I'd like to elucidate the distinction by drawing on another era of American film: the film noir of the late 40s and early 50s.

The big, dumb, blunt interventions of the bureaucrat high modernists are equivalent to the 80s action movies with their big, dumb, muscle-bound heroes running around with bazookas blowing the enemy to smithereens. 'Smash the curve' is the perfect mantra for an 80s action movie where a lot of smashing and bashing goes on. That works OK when the bad guys are 100% bad and get exactly what they deserve. It doesn't work in the real world. In the real world there is ambiguity and complexity. That ambiguity and complexity is far better captured by film noir. Unlike the 80s action hero, the classic film noir hero is a conflicted person with his own inner demons that are exacerbated by the social context in which he or she finds himself. There is no right and wrong for such a hero, just shades of grey. That conflicted, imperfect hero is often juxtaposed against a rabid mob. This was a favourite trope of the German director Fritz Lang who had, after all, witnessed the dynamic first hand as he watched Hitler come to power. Naturally, mobs are not easy to reason with and it's up to the protagonist to fight back against them.

One of the greatest of the film noirs is the movie *Boomerang*, directed by Elia Kazan. It features exactly this dynamic of a conflicted protagonist trying to neutralise an irrational mob. In the movie, a callous and cowardly murder has taken place in a small city in America. The townsfolk are horrified and demand the murderer be brought to justice immediately. However, the police have no good leads and results are not forthcoming. Frustration grows and political pressure is exerted on the chief of police to find the culprit quickly. Still no good leads are found but eventually they come across a suspect whose alibi is weak and, although he maintains his innocence, they force a confession out of him.

The case goes to the district attorney who is a handsome, competent and popular man with a beautiful wife and a wonderful life ahead of him. The matter is as straightforward as can be. A suspect has confessed. Everybody in town wants him to be found guilty. All the district attorney has to do is run through the motions. But the district attorney is a man of honour. He checks the evidence and sees that it doesn't add up. In a dramatic twist he declares that he believes the man innocent at which point he is taken aside by the powers that be and presented with a series of carrots and eventually sticks to get him to do what is wanted. His final choice is clear: he can pursue justice and have his life ruined or he can acquiesce to the mob and continue his rise through the ranks of the elite.

The heroism presented in this case is the heroism to pursue what you know to be right even though the society around you will forsake you. Anybody can follow along with what the mob wants, especially when it calls you a hero. But the deeper heroism is to do what is right though you will be condemned for it. The reason why this is specifically relevant in the case of the corona event is because most of the people working in the medical and scientific fields are compromised by the fact that they make their living either directly or indirectly from government and/or the medical industry. The corona event has seen a flood of new money go into the biomedical fields for research, vaccines, PCR tests, hospitals and all the rest. This gives the people who work in those areas a very strong incentive not to speak out against what is happening. To speak out requires exactly the kind of bravery and heroism presented in the movie Boomerang. It's to do what is right even though it will hurt your life chances. We have seen exactly that kind of heroism during the corona event but it has mostly taken place on the fringes and has been explicitly excluded from the mainstream media.

One of the surprising and disappointing factors in the corona event has been the failure of the institutions in our society to provide at least one alternative viewpoint on what is happening. This was especially true in the early stages. In Australia there has been absolutely nothing from opposition political parties, the mainstream media or the scientific and medical establishment. Apparently, we have a complete consensus here on the path forward even though it's obvious that path forward has changed almost daily and our politicians are making it up as they go. We could barely muster a single dissenting voice that mattered. Lesser voices were quickly put down via the usual social media mob mentality that Fritz Lang would recognise. Fortunately, in this age of the internet we are not restricted by national boundaries and so dissenting voices from other countries are available to us. One particular dissenting voice from overseas captured my attention: Professor Sucharit Bhakdi, a professor of medical microbiology and apparently one of the foremost in Germany. Bhakdi went public because he saw what was happening made no sense from a scientific point of view let alone a moral point of view. Why Bhakdi is even more interesting though is because he was born in Thailand and only recently became a citizen of Germany because he wanted to live in a democracy. Unlike the rest of us who take democracy so much for granted that we are happy to put it on hold, apparently indefinitely, Bhakdi reacted with horror as he watched democracy be thrown out the window. The fact that it was done on the pretence of science that didn't make sense to him was just the icing on the cake. Bhakdi filled the role we have just identified in the film noir. An insider who understands how the system works and sees that system betraying its own ideals to pander to a mob.

That is my kind of heroism. The heroism to speak against a stifling consensus. Incidentally, it's also the job of the true scientist. Where have been the other scientists to speak out? Even Bhakdi lamented that his own students (of which there are apparently many thousands) have remained silent. No doubt they are worried for their careers. No doubt many of them are happy to play the role of doctor-as-hero or scientist-as-hero that our society has created for them. But the true scientific hero is the kind of person like Professor Bhakdi. Is it just a coincidence that Germany seems to be one of the few countries where some citizens are protesting against the measures being put in place? At least there they have somebody to give an alternative view based on science.

To return to the movie Boomerang, the district attorney does save the day and he does so in a dramatic gimmick in the courtroom that proves beyond a doubt that the defendant is innocent. Unfortunately, we are not going to get such a certain proof with the corona event. This is the real world and not the movies. There is no smoking gun evidence that is going to change people's minds. The desire for heroism early on in the corona event quickly morphed into a high modernist, 80s action movie hero dynamic. Just like an 80s action movie, there's going to be collateral damage all over the place. The only question at the moment seems to be, how much?

Most of that damage is going to be economic and, if the last couple of decades is any indication, that economic damage is likely to work its way into politics too. In the next chapter I want to look at how the economics of globalisation played a role in the lead up to the corona event. Then, in the final chapter, we will bring together some of the higher level themes of this book as we look at how the corona event fits within the dominant ethos of modern western society: heroic materialism.

Chapter 9: The Economics of Corona

At the time of writing (September, 2020), the city where I live, Melbourne, Australia, has been in what is now one of the longest and hardest lockdowns of any city in the world. This despite the fact that the number of infections here is very low by international standards. Victoria, and by extension Australia, fell backwards into a situation where 'elimination' of the virus seemed possible and the achievement of that goal became the strategy more by luck than good management. As per the seemingly random nature of the virus elsewhere, Victoria had an outbreak which the rest of the country avoided and then one thing led to another until finally political conditions here came to make North Korea look like a bastion of freedom and democracy. Readers may have seen some of the images which have now spread around the world and no doubt put a nice dent in the reputation of a city that for so long prided itself on being the world's 'most liveable'.

Unexpectedly, then, Melbourne has become ground zero for many of the themes in this book. For that reason, I think going over some of the economic developments that have been happening here over the last couple of decades is going to be relevant to the larger direction of this book. I had been watching those developments first-hand with a combination of interest and consternation. Most social change is very slow and therefore happens quite invisibly. But things were changing so quickly in Melbourne that the effects of that change were very noticeable and they were having a direct impact on my life and the lives of others. The official position was that everything was going great. The economy was booming and Australia was considered some kind of economic wunderkind as we hadn't had a recession in decades. From my position on the ground, that didn't add up. We were swimming in cash but much of what was going on had a self-evidently detrimental impact on the quality of life for citizens on the ground.

Firstly, public transport had become intolerable. Overseas readers, especially those in the US, should note that in Australian capital cities it is normal for most people to take public transport and in particular the salary class uses public transport to commute to work as most salary class jobs are in the CBD. People would show up to work complaining about how they had to wait three trains before they could even get on and if you managed to get on you were crammed in like a sardine.

Secondly, traffic had become so bad that the time it took to drive some place had in some cases doubled or even tripled. Many people I know who commuted by car told stories of how a drive that would have taken twenty minutes on an uncongested road, would usually take over an hour. That's an extra hour and half every day of the week sitting in a car just to get to and from work. I didn't drive a lot but whenever I had to drive anywhere during business hours I was stunned how bad the traffic was and wondered how anybody, in particular tradesmen and other people who made their living driving around, put up with it.

The last refuge, the one good way to get around Melbourne, was cycling. As an enthusiastic bike rider, I had always made use of this form of transport whenever possible. But in the Melbourne CBD the footpaths had become so full that pedestrians were walking on the road. As the cycling path is right next to the footpath, this meant that the bike lanes were now full of people. Although I try to be polite when on my bike, many Melbourne bike riders are notoriously rude and I saw many incidents of cyclists screaming at pedestrians to get out of their way.

The root cause of all this was, of course, population growth. Far from this being seen as a problem, the media crowed about how Melbourne would soon be 'bigger than Sydney' and that we were bursting at the seams. The growth in population had other side effects. The price of real estate, both to rent and buy, had reached absurd heights that were so unsustainable that it became something of a sport to try and predict when the bubble would pop. The overcrowding due to population growth also spilled over into office life and this leads me to a story that relates specifically to the corona event.

I got a new job in an office. I should say upfront that the quality of offices in Melbourne had long been a bugbear of mine. They are usually dingy and drab but, more importantly from a health point of view, the ventilation in them is awful. Usually the windows don't even open and there is some antiquated HVAC system from the 1950s pumping god knows what through the vents. Even the newer offices featured HVAC systems designed for low energy usage rather than for effectiveness. The office at my new job was a good example of the type of problem I'm talking about. Some split systems had been tacked onto to an old building and that was the extent of the HVAC system. The windows in the office did open. But, apparently, I was the only one who wanted them open. After a few instances of me opening a window only to have it closed again shortly after, I gave up. People didn't seem to like fresh air. Maybe it reminded them that there was a big beautiful world outside and they were stuck in an office.

Winter rolled around and, inevitably, people started to get sick. Now, bear in mind that in Australian culture prior to the corona event, you only stayed home from work if you were really sick and couldn't work or if you were pretending to be sick and were really going to the beach. If you had a cough and a runny nose, it was expected that you would come to work and nobody had the slightest problem with it. At one point in mid-winter, the office resembled a hospital ward. I counted how many people were coughing and sneezing. It was about 80% of the people. Not just cough here and a sneeze there. All day long. Finally, I too succumbed and had to spend three days in bed with a fever. This was particularly annoying for me because it occurred over the weekend, which is bad enough, but I also moonlight as a musician and had a particularly juicy gig on the weekend in question. I had to miss the gig and so I was more than a little grumpy about the situation. A respiratory virus had infected everybody in the office. You didn't need any advanced laboratory tests to prove it. It was plain to the naked eye. But here's the thing: nobody cared. There were a couple of comments about the 'bad flu year' and people just got on with their lives.

Why did the illness spread so easily in that office? Well, for one it was overcrowded. The company had grown strongly and there had been a lot of rearranging of furniture to fit as many people as possible in. As I've already stated, there was no proper ventilation. And, of course, everybody in the office travelled to work on overcrowded public transport meaning all manner of potential germs were tracked into an office where they had the perfect incubator-like environment. Again, all this was business as usual at the time. If you had pointed these facts out to people back then they might have thought you were a hypochondriac or just a whinger.

What all this amounts to is inflation. Good quality HVAC systems cost money. Renting office space costs money. I don't blame the people in charge of the company because our culture prior to the corona event simply paid no attention to these kinds of things and so they were an uncontroversial way to cut costs. Nevertheless, it was clear to me that this cost cutting was at the expense of employee welfare. From the employee's point of view, if I don't have enough personal space at work and on the train getting to work and if that lack of space makes me more likely to get sick, that's a small but not insignificant reduction in my quality of life.

There were other, more blatant examples, of cost cutting at the expense of employee welfare which became popular in large corporates in the last decade or so. My favourite was the hot desk movement. For those who haven't been exposed to this wonderful innovation, it means you don't have your own desk at the office. Each day you show up for work, collect your things from a locker and try to find somewhere to sit. Supposedly this was all about encouraging employee communication. In reality, it's about cramming more employees into the same floor space. Even the official justifications admitted this fact. We were told how, given you have X% of people either sick or on leave on any given day, there was 'wasted' floor space that didn't get used. Why not turn that wasted floor space into money for the company? Of course, hot desking is inconvenient for employees. In the best-case scenario, you have to haul your stuff to a locker twice a day. In the more dysfunctional organisations, it often meant you simply couldn't get a place to sit. I recall one particularly dysfunctional company where the bean counters obviously screwed up their calculations because there were simply not enough desks and the result was a constant battle to try and find somewhere for team members to sit. Literally hours a week were wasted on this activity by a large number of employees which must have had a big negative impact on productivity and employee morale. Of course, the managers making the decisions were not rewarded on these metrics but on savings to the rent. In economic jargon, the costs were being externalised and they were being externalised onto us as employees.

This externalisation of costs is exactly what has happened in the last couple of decades (and arguably longer than that) in society as a whole. The trends in transportation that I mentioned above are also an externalised cost. Once upon a time, you could pay for a train ticket and get a seat. Then you couldn't get a seat and had to stand. Then you had to stand crowded in with other people. Then you could barely get on. Finally, you couldn't even get on. Each step along that path is inflation but it's not the kind of inflation that gets counted in the official statistics. In fact, the statistics are usually changed so they ignore just these kinds of problem. In one of the more comedic examples of that, a study was done on overcrowding in Melbourne trams. It found not very much overcrowding which was surely a surprise to anybody who had actually tried to use public transport at the time. What was the definition of an 'overcrowded tram' used in the study? Well, if you could get on the tram, then it wasn't overcrowded. With a wave of the definitional wand, the problem was made to disappear from the official record. The official statistics also don't count the amount of time you have to spend in your car to get from A to B or the fact that your bike ride now involves trying not to run over pedestrians or the fact that ventilation system where you work is nothing more than a glorified germ dispersion unit. In the last two decades, all of this hidden inflation was going on alongside very obvious forms of inflation in the real estate market.

With the corona event, all this invisible inflation has come to the fore in the most spectacular fashion. Overcrowding, high density accommodation, tourism, the immigration-higher education-real estate bubble that has propped up the Australian economy for decades, cheap buildings and offices, just in time logistics, high debt levels etc. It turns out that almost everything that has been source of hidden inflation over the past decades has had to be shut down. Tourism and immigration have stopped. Higher education (and all education for that matter) continues on but in a debased, online form. Nobody's buying real estate. There's no overcrowding on public transport anymore; nobody takes it. There's no traffic anymore; nobody is driving. Nobody is going to the cheap, overcrowded offices with shoddy ventilation systems; they are 'working' from home. Nobody is even going to hospital or doctors any more. In many countries, medical workers were furloughed due to lack of work. Emergency departments were empty. Sometimes that led to real problems such as people avoiding treatment for what became serious conditions. But clearly a lot of those hospital and doctor visits that happened in the past simply didn't need to happen. People seem to get by without them now.

The trends described above were no accident. As I alluded to in chapter six, social changes in the past couple of decades had the effect of increasing the movement of people and therefore, in theory, the spread of communicable disease. These trends were part of the policy which we might as well call globalisation but could also call neo-liberalism. A core tenet of globalisation is the free movement of people. In countries like Australia, that free movement of people manifested as a large increase in population. That's why you couldn't get on a train. That's why you couldn't walk on the footpath. That's why there were so many people in the office. This kind of inflation is caused by simply increasing the supply of money. In Australia, this was done quite explicitly. The immigration system was heavily tilted towards bringing in people with money either directly or through an indirect payment such as the higher education system. Economics 101 says that if you increase the amount of money relative to the supply of goods and services in an economy, you get inflation. That's a simple law of economics but we weren't measuring real inflation and so we convinced ourselves that inflation was really growth.

The free movement of people is a core part of the doctrine of globalisation but, as it turns out, the free movement of people is also the free movement of communicable disease. Nobody gave it a second thought prior to the corona event, but everybody now knows how personal behaviour apparently contributes to viral disease. We are told to keep distance and wash our hands, for example. But there's been no talk about how our lifestyles, the lifestyles at the centre of globalisation, have changed the spread of communicable disease. In the last two decades, we travelled all around the world, exposing our body to new germs everywhere we went and bringing our own germs to new people and locations. We crammed onto public transport. We went to work while sick. People actually went on cruise ships. Tell that to your grandchildren because the cruise ship industry may be one that doesn't survive for posterity. Nobody gave any of this a second thought. All this behaviour which would now be considered risky at best and murderous at worst was apparently no problem prior to corona. But it's become a big problem now, even if the problem is mostly psychological. The policy of globalisation seems to have run face first into what would seem to be a brick wall of insurmountable proportions. In the mind of the public, the free movement of people is now the same thing as a public health catastrophe. And yet the debate hasn't borne that out. In fact, we have already seen the first scramblings to try and put humpty dumpty back together. All the king's horses and all the king's men seemed to have been waiting for just this exact thing to happen. The same people that brought us globalisation also set up the early warning signal that has triggered the corona event. That's why they also did us all the favour of coming up with the solution in advance: social distancing, masks and vaccines.

Setting aside whether these measures actually 'work', from an economic point of view (a *real* economic point of view not a bunch of statistics and abstractions) they represent exactly the same kind of inflation I have been talking about in this post. The wearing of a mask, for example, is the most obvious kind of inflation. Despite desperate attempts by some people to convince themselves otherwise, wearing a mask sucks. It is uncomfortable and unpleasant in the most basic physiological sense let alone the psychological, political and symbolic elements to it. To have to wear a mask is the exact same kind of inflation as cramming onto public transport or having to sit in your car an extra five hours a week. It's simply disagreeable. But here in Melbourne as in many others places, we have been putting up with the cramming onto public transport for the last ten years. We have been putting up with not being able to walk on the footpath. We have been putting up with the endless traffic jams. We have been conditioned to accept just this kind of inflation. Part of that conditioning was to not call it inflation. Rather, we called it 'growth' and 'progress'. This is the same trick that was pulled by corporates saying hot desking was about 'enhanced communication'. It the same tick that is being pulled now with phrases like 'the new normal'.

Logically, this new normal shouldn't even get to the starting gate. What is being promised is all the problems that were there before only now you get masks and vaccines on top of it. You'll still have your miserable commute only now you get to wear a mask too. We won't do anything to solve the underlying spread of communicable disease, we'll just give you more and more vaccines. Really, it's all just inflation dressed up as progress. But, as I have been at pains to point out in this book, stories and myths need not be related to actual results and the more powerful and deep seated a myth the more disconnected from reality it can become. What's important with myths is that they are told and re-told. The myth of progress has been getting told here in Melbourne at exactly the same time when the results on the ground have not borne it out. We have been going backwards economically while telling ourselves we were progressing. That (real) economic decline has been having political consequences in both the UK and the USA but Australia managed to avoid it. Until now. If I'm reading it correctly, the corona event will represent the time when the chickens come home to roost here also.

The way myths work is that you can get away with not delivering results for a time. Perhaps even a long time. In fact, societies have collapsed entirely through an inability to change their myths. The myth of progress hasn't been delivering the goods for quite some time now. We still don't have our hoverboards or our flying cars. We still haven't gone to Mars or done many of the other things that was once predicted. What seems to be happening now is that the myth of progress itself is being reworked to fit the absence of results. Once upon a time, progress meant flying cars and hoverboards. Now it means facemasks and social distancing. Once upon a time, vaccines liberated people from inevitable disease. Now apparently society must be put on hold completely until a vaccine is procured. You can call that progress and you can get away with it for quite a long time but eventually people will start to realise something is up and eventually reality might intervene.

Will it be possible to convince people that masks, social distancing and vaccines really do represent progress? A heroic advance to conquer infectious disease once and for all? It seems very unlikely that this could happen mostly because these measures will also have a significant dampening on economic activity and that is where the rubber will hit the road. But there is something larger at play in this case and that something is, in fact, the founding ethos of modern western civilisation. The economic developments in Melbourne I have outlined above are not coincidental. What we have done in the last two decades is build roads, bridges, tunnels, skyscrapers and desalinisation plants. This is nothing fundamentally different from what we were doing one hundred years ago. Such projects are paradigm examples of the heroic materialism of the industrial revolution. And so, the last few decades have in some ways been the re-assertion of that heroic materialism as the dominant narrative of our society. I don't believe it is a coincidence that the corona event took the political trajectory that it did in Melbourne. The high modernist response we have seen fits with the myth of progress and with the heroic materialism that has been going on all around us for the last two decades. The corona event shows that we are still operating under that pattern. In fact, it's more than a pattern. It's an identity. In the next and final chapter of this book, we'll take a look at heroic materialism and whether the corona event can prompt us to re-evaluate some of the defining elements of our culture.

Chapter 10: Beyond Heroic Materialism

Perhaps the main question for those of us who are baffled by how we got stuck in the mess that is the corona event was asked by the German microbiologist Bhakdi: how could a society of educated people allow this to happen? Surely the whole point of having a democracy with educated citizens is so that robust public debate can occur and multiple viewpoints be taken into consideration?

There is no single answer to Bhakdi's question. I have tried to cover the main points as I see it in this book. To recapitulate, I believe the primary reason is that in February-March there was a battle in the public discourse between two competing narratives: the plague story or the flu story. For the reasons sketched out in this book and some others I have no doubt missed, the plague story won. But that only changes the question to: how could a society of educated people convince themselves they were in a plague story when it should have been clear they weren't? The willingness with which most people accepted the plague story seemingly without any scepticism explains Bhakdi's surprise. By 'educated', he means educated in science. Educated to ask questions and interrogate the data. (I'll set aside here a discussion around whether our education system doesn't produce the exact opposite of this attitude). This is one of the prime assumptions of our society: we are scientific. Ironically, this is just another story and is, in fact, one of the founding myths of modern society: we are above stories; we are scientific.

The idea that we are above stories is no accident. We are still heirs to The Enlightenment which was in large part the battle between science and story in the form of the revolt against religion. It is no small irony that this movement began in the person of Isaac Newton who spent more time trying to fix the inconsistencies in the Bible than he did working on his scientific breakthroughs. Nevertheless, it was his work on planetary orbits that started a revolution and is widely considered to be the real beginning of western science. Newton's genius is probably understood by fewer people nowadays than it was in his time. It was what we can call *reductionist science*. Specifically, in relation to calculating the motions of the planets, Newton was able to achieve this by simplifying the number of calculations involved through a series of brilliant assumptions. The method was reductionist because of all the things it left out of consideration. It was only by reducing the number of variables that the calculations could be solved. To say that this approach was revolutionary is possibly an understatement. Most serious thinkers from that time on wanted to be reductionists. Philosophers such as Kant were inspired to create great systems of philosophy while scientists got to work creating powerful generalisations that were testable and reproducible. The idea was to simplify everything down to what could be calculated. This allowed predictions to be made and rules to be generated. Those rules could be relied on to produce results. One of those results was the creation of society as we know it. I will describe the ethos of that society, borrowing the title from the final episode of Kenneth Clark's wonderful 1969 TV series *Civilisation*, as Heroic Materialism.

Heroic Materialism involves reductionist science but is mostly about the industrial revolution which had its own momentum in the development of technology and the relentless ramping up of capitalism as the organising principle of society. This eventually led to the radical reshaping of our world in railways, tunnels, roads, cars, dams, bridges and skyscrapers. In science, it culminated in a giddy period toward the end of the 19th century where scientists firmly believed that before long the whole world would be explicable in terms of generalisations and calculations. Everything would be predictable. Everything would be within the control of man. It was around that time when the breakthroughs in infectious disease also started to be made. As with the increasing control man had over his environment, it seemed that for the first-time real inroads could be made in relation to disease which, until then, had been seen as simply an inevitable part of life. Improvements in water quality, sewerage, general sanitation and, of course, vaccines led to a massive reduction in mortality from infectious disease. These gains continued up until around the late 1960s when, as mentioned in previous chapters, the US Surgeon General in 1967 declared it time to close the book on infectious disease. No wonder then that people at the time were optimistic[1].

We look back on that enthusiasm and optimism with gentle mockery because we know all too well what came next. The world wars where the machines of the industrial revolution were used to create human misery on an almost unimaginable scale. The atomic bomb where for the first-time man appeared to have the power to destroy not just himself but the whole planet. And the environmental degradation which had always gone hand in glove with the industrial revolution but which became an immediate fact of daily life. It's astonishing to think that, in some of the largest cities in the world, smog used to cause mass death. In a four day period in London in 1952, somewhere between 4,000 and 12,000 people died from a 'killer fog'[2]. In Los Angeles around the same time, the smog was so bad that schools were closed for a whole month. New York and other cities had similar incidents. These were, of course, just a continuation of the pollution that had been around right since the start of the industrial revolution. As with the health crises and rampant poverty of the 19th century, there was pushback to the growing pollution problems in the form of the nascent environmentalist movement which played the same role that the romantics played in relation to the beginning of bourgeois ascendancy at the start of the industrial revolution i.e. a critique of things that seemed absurdly bad and yet nobody really paid attention to. This seeming indifference to suffering had been a part of heroic materialism since the start as witnessed by the large numbers of deaths on big projects and the general misery and squalor in which working class people lived during much of the 19th century in Britain and elsewhere.

Why did people put up with it? You could argue they made a cost/benefit analysis and reasoned that the benefits of industrialisation outweighed the costs, just as some people now might say that the benefits of the corona lockdown outweigh the costs. I don't believe that's true. The cost/benefit analysis implies an objectivity that simply doesn't exist. What's at stake in these matters are values. People don't say the costs outweigh the benefits. They reject the costs altogether. The costs are simply excluded from consideration. Pollution was simply ignored until it couldn't be ignored anymore. When smog kills thousands of people in one day (and presumably makes a great many more very sick), it's really hard to continue to argue that you don't have a problem. That's simply the way it works with human beings. We usually need to be dragged kicking and screaming away from our addictions.

A similar process happens in science where, as the saying goes, progress happens one funeral at a time. A new theory starts off with a bang and represents a genuine breakthrough. Enthusiasm spikes and people start to make use of the new framework. The early results look great as all the low hanging fruit gets picked. Over time, the results slow to a trickle and the deficiencies and shortcomings (costs) start to mount. The deficiencies get explained away until the burden becomes so great that a paradigm shift comes along and the process starts over again. There is a natural conservatism at play in human affairs. Once something has 'worked', we become very reluctant to even admit its failings.

Assuming that the benefits of heroic materialism did outweigh the costs at the start, it was around the middle of the 20th century that the accrual of those benefits noticeably began to slow. There was still the moon landing to come and some last strains of optimism, including the statement in 1954 that the rolling out of nuclear power would produce electricity that was 'too cheap to meter'. Unfortunately, that cheap power never showed up. Neither did our flying cars or our hoverboards. Those failures, usually covered up in the form of jokes and light cynicism, have become more pressing in recent times. Let's take the issue of health. In the last several decades, there has been essentially no further reduction in infectious disease mortality despite more money being spent on the issue[3]. The US Surgeon General in 1967 was right; all the easy gains had been made. He was also right in saying that we should shift focus to combating lifestyle disease. But that hasn't happened. Instead, there has been a relentless rise in cases of diabetes and other lifestyle illnesses leading to the fact that, for the first time in generations, average life expectancy has declined in the West. On the economic front, things have also been going backwards. In the 1970s, the average family could live fairly comfortably on a single wage. Nowadays that would be impossible in most western nations. I addressed these economic issues in the previous chapter so I won't repeat them here.

Those who still want to talk up heroic materialism nowadays usually do so in relation to what we can call globalisation. For example, the increased expenditure on western medicine in Africa and, of course, the big one: China. If ever there was a poster child for heroic materialism, it would be modern China. We've heard all about the number of people pulled out of poverty there. We've seen the pictures of massive bridges and dams and skyscrapers. We've also heard about the environmental degradation too. Nevertheless, China is the big example to show that heroic materialism can still deliver the goods.

I wonder if the corona event isn't partly driven by a desire to see heroic materialism once again deliver the goods here in the west. As we saw in chapter eight, there was a clear desire for heroism from the public. Perhaps the reason we needed heroics and heroism was precisely because heroic materialism has been failing to deliver for quite some time. Maybe people intuit in some general sense that the system that is western civilisation isn't working properly anymore and really does need saving by a hero. Simple pragmatism wasn't going to cut it in this case. In fact, pragmatism in general has been cast aside and we are in a weird kind of twilight zone where nothing else matters but the virus. Economic considerations, psychological issues, civil liberties, even the business of sending children to school has all become subservient to that one end.

This obsessive focus is a prime feature of both scientific reductionism and heroic materialism. It is also a feature of James C. Scott's high modernist intervention; a type of intervention predicated on bureaucracy, which is the organisational type most associated with heroic materialism.

It is probably hard for us to believe nowadays, but bureaucracy was once seen as a big advance and also came to the fore during the optimism of the end of the 19th century. Bureaucracy was perceived as a kind of machine that ran on rules rather than the old systems of cronyism and nepotism. Just like reductionist science, corporations and bureaucracies owe their power and efficacy to focus. In the case of a corporation, it means reducing all discussion down to profit and loss. Whatever else can be said about that, it gives a clear and somewhat objective way to resolve issues and align energies within the organisation. Of course, we've all had the experience of having to deal with a bureaucracy that's too busy focusing on the thing that *it* thinks matters and is unable to focus on the thing that *we* think matters. And we all know the stories of corporations so focused on the bottom line that they pollute the environment or even sacrifice human life as a consequence. There are drawbacks to focus. The high modernist interventions described by Scott featured bureaucracies focused on simplistic metrics who were unable to respond to real world feedback. Thus, we now see western governments floundering around with all kinds of seemingly arbitrary restrictions aimed at 'controlling' the virus. How many people are allowed to congregate. What time of the evening is curfew. On what grounds may one cross a border. That one has to wear a mask while being seated in a restaurant but after that may take it off to eat (but must put it back on when the waiter comes to the table). As Kafka pointed out, arbitrary rules pretending to be based in reason is what bureaucracy has always produced. The corona event represents just that kind of old-fashioned, bureaucratic intervention that we've seen fail time and again. Just like the interventions described by Scott, it focuses relentlessly and exclusively on a single metric: infections. No surprise, of course, that it has been run out of the public health bureaucracies which are just the kind of organisations to fall into that kind of error. In the public and in the media, the underlying story is the naïve germ theory which reduces everything down to the virus. Nothing else matters.

So, another way to frame the question about the corona event is: why have we lapsed back into the kind of high modernist, reductionist, bureaucratic mindset that almost the entire 20th century showed us does not work?

The most obvious answer is: we have never got beyond that mindset. We are still heroic materialists. This is, in fact, exactly what Kenneth Clark pointed out back in 1969. With the failure of Marxism, heroic materialism became the only game in town. (We should, however, note that Marxism was also firmly predicated on the myth of science and so the main difference was in economic systems). The reason why this is not obvious to us is precisely because of that other myth that is central to our worldview: the myth of progress. By definition, we must have progressed beyond where we once were because more time has elapsed. The logic is irrefutable but, as I showed in the last chapter, the truth is the opposite. We have simply been telling ourselves the myth that we have been progressing without bothering to either to define what progress really means or check that we are, in fact, progressing. Kind of strange for a society that prides itself on measuring and controlling things.

What if the corona event really represents a regression? An economic regression is an incontrovertible fact right now and the only question is how much of a regression it will be. But what if the regression is wider than that? What if it's also a political and cultural regression? One way to explore this idea is by a distinction made by Theodore Roszak who classified western societies as *suave technocracies* in contrast to China, Russia and others which were *vulgar technocracies*. The underlying structure of the technocracy (expertise, bureaucracy and 'science') is shared between these societies. What is different is the sophistication of western nations and most of that sophistication was provided by democracy and the free market both of which allow for other perspectives to balance out the single-minded focus of the technocrat. Under this analysis, what has happened in the west during the corona event is simply that the suave, fashionable gloves came off and we reverted to vulgar technocracy. That's why the corona event has all the hallmarks of the high modernist intervention that we had previously seen in Russia and China in the 20th century. This was done through the various states of emergency which had the effect of shutting down civil society, democracy and the free market and left us with just government to run the show. As governments operate through bureaucracy, the problem was translated into the simplistic terms that a bureaucracy can handle: infections. Looked at this way, what we have seen during the corona event is the bare bones of heroic materialism stripped of all subtlety and nuance. That the whole thing began in China is an irony for the history books. It was vulgar technocracy that turned out to be infectious. It is this fact that is behind the sting that comes from the knowledge that here in Melbourne, for example, we have had a longer lockdown than in Wuhan. Those of us who shook our heads and marvelled at what was going in Wuhan in January now shake our heads and marvel at our own society.

Translated into these terms, the desire for heroism seen during the corona event was perhaps borne out of a frustration with intricacies and delicacies of the suave technocracy. We wanted the 80s action hero to come in with his muscles and his bazookas to save the day. The whole point of our civilisation is that we can 'smash' a virus. So, that's what we must do. If I'm right, then we are in for an interesting period because, to use a well-known meme: *one does not simply smash a virus*. Just like the high modernist interventions of the past, the simplifying model does not work in the real world.

At time of writing, we are entering a period of death by a thousand cuts as government bureaucracies heap rules onto a baffled public. That's going to cause growing frustration the longer it goes on for. Governments have already poured billions into a vaccine because that's the standard way to end a modern plague story. However, a vaccine is highly unlikely to the provide the closure that will so desperately be desired. For starters, the vaccine may take years. If the vaccine gets rushed through, there may be health side effects. Then there is the question of whether the vaccine will even work at all. Then there is the fact that the amount of attention placed on this vaccine will be enormous, especially if governments try to make it mandatory. As a result, any negative side effects are likely to be well publicised. If pharmaceutical companies get legal waivers for those side effects, the blowback will go straight to government.

That's just the vaccine part of the story. The economic effects, still yet to really hit home, would have to be enormous at this point. Once again, it seems the only option governments are going to have is to print money to try and get spending back to where it was. Will that work? How are borders going to be re-opened again? How is international travel going to happen? There are stories of vaccine passports and similar measures but they represent a tax on all travel and economics 101 says that when the price goes up the demand goes down. What does globalisation look like if people can't travel around? There is an idea popular among certain groups that we can simply detach globalisation and return to national heroic materialism. That might be possible in some places although I think people underestimate how complex global manufacturing has become and how hard it would be to unwind. There has been some talk of massive infrastructure spending to get the economy going and no doubt there will be other schemes. Even if we were to achieve this to some level of success, is it something that people could be optimistic about? It's likely to feel a lot like treading water. Is what we really need more roads, more bridges, more tunnels? Here in Melbourne I can say quite categorically we do not. We've been building plenty of those for the last two decades and it hasn't made things any better. If the corona event represents the re-assertion of heroic materialism, it's very hard to see how it is going to be a 'success'. Maybe it's time once again to try a re-evaluation of the whole concept. If the corona event represents a failure of heroic materialism and high modernist ideology, what other options are on the table?

Reductive science, bureaucracy and corporations get their power mostly from focus. You ignore 'non-essential' factors and concentrate only on what produces the result you are looking for. But focus has drawbacks among which are the possibility that you don't *really* want the result you are looking for and that you might get some other results you didn't think about. Once again, I refer to Richard Feynman because he told one of the most poignant stories about the problems with focus, specifically in relation to the development of the H Bomb at Los Alamos. The initial reason given to the scientists for the development of the bomb was to beat the Germans to it. But, after the Germans surrendered in May 1945, the scientists kept working on the bomb even though that initial reason was no longer valid. It simply didn't occur to anybody to stop. They were too close to the finish line and everybody wanted to get the result. They got a result, of course: the bomb got dropped on Japan. Feynman, like many others at that time, went into a deep depression for a couple of years afterwards firmly convinced that humans would destroy themselves with the bomb. He told of how he lamented that they didn't cancel the project when the Germans surrendered. That they didn't de-focus and re-evaluate what they were doing.

This kind of error is exactly what James C. Scott talked about in relation to high modernism. It is the same error committed by corporations which focus exclusively on profit at the expense of everything else or bureaucracies who are unable to react to real world feeback. We are committing exactly the same error right now with an obsessive focus on 'infections' at the expense of every other consideration. I have already mentioned one body of work which dealt with these kinds of errors, Gerald Weinberg's *General Systems Thinking*. Weinberg's solution to excessive focus is quite straightforward: you must allow multiple perspectives to be heard. You must be able to de-focus as well as focus. To step back and see the bigger picture. Indeed, you must force yourself to do so in order that you don't fall into just these kind of traps. You must also be aware of what you are simplifying by stating your assumptions and doing what Feynman suggested: trying to prove *yourself* wrong or at least thinking about if you could be wrong. Ideally, a functioning civil society in a democracy should achieve these outcomes through public discourse and the parliamentary process.

Weinberg's work was practical in nature but around the same time there were also philosophical challenges to heroic materialism and these came from within science itself. In her wonderful book, *The Myths we Live By*, Mary Midgley talks about how the Enlightenment ideal of the social contract was influenced by the physics of that time. The notion of solitary, self-contained, selfish individuals in the political realm was an analogue to the focus on atoms as the basic particles of existence. These ideas continued right through Darwin with his emphasis of competition in nature and into works like Dawkins with his selfish gene. Is it a coincidence that with the lockdowns during the corona event we have all been reduced back down to solitary, self-contained creatures in our own homes? Our Enlightenment social contract has been suspended and we've reverted back to little, self-contained atoms. Is it also a coincidence that our naïve germ theory has the exact attitude to viruses and bacteria that Dawkins has about genes i.e. as ruthless gangsters; selfish, brutish, pernicious. Of course, physics hasn't been concerned with atoms or particles for over a hundred years. The idea that individual particles are fundamental is no longer valid there. It looks like microbiology will eventually get to a similar place. We now know that viruses and bacteria are not necessarily the enemy and that we are in fact reliant on some of them for our health and well-being. Modern science is showing us that connections and relationships are at least as fundamental as 'objects' and, in fact, the whole idea of an object independent of an observer doesn't make much sense. If Enlightenment physics influenced Enlightenment political thought, modern science should be able to prompt for a re-evaluation of our own politics and our own world view.

This could be true if, as Professor Bhakdi assumed, educated people made an attempt to think through the ramifications of modern science and use that as a prompt for philosophical re-evaluation. Something like that has happened, for example, with the attempt to use quantum mechanics to establish the idea of free will. But in general it has not happened. The findings of modern science have not seeped through into the general culture. Why not? Part of the reason, I believe, is the fact that a scientist is now a salaried employee rather than an independent thinker. This means that scientists have become experts in sub-sub-sub disciplines and either can't or don't know how to relate their work back to larger social and philosophical problems. By contrast, the heroic scientists were usually Renaissance men and women rather than specialists. They had no difficulty in seeing the relevance of their work to the larger culture. Darwin, for example, knew perfectly well what kind of bomb would get set off by the publishing of his theories. So much so that he had organised for publication to happen after his death but changed his mind when Wallace came forward with the same ideas.

There may also be specific reasons why findings from microbiology would be problematic for the larger culture. These findings challenge longstanding beliefs in the west over the separation of man from nature and go directly against the trend of biophobia that I outlined in chapter nine. But biophobia also has larger roots in the culture. Midgley notes that this antipathy to nature goes back to Christianity and specifically in the battle fought between the church and nature religions at different points in its history. It's also the case that for much of western history, nature has been the equivalent to chaos. It was, by definition, the thing which could not be understood. That's why we spent so much time star gazing because at least the sky offered a regularity and objectivity that was reassuring. The idea that the earth is inherently degraded or sinful also has deep roots in Christianity. It wasn't until breakthroughs in geology and then the Darwinian revolution that our perspective started to change and we could try and make sense of nature from within science. By explicitly positing the relation between humans and animals, Darwin also began to breakdown the longstanding belief in humans as something apart from nature. This was, indeed, what the romantics had already been getting at. But the romantics lost the argument and we chose heroic materialism instead. Heroic materialism is predicated on a domination of nature and systematically filters out anything that does not fit with that model.

It wasn't until the mid-20th century, when the drawbacks of heroic materialism had become unavoidable, that there was another re-evaluation and I have mentioned one exponent of that, Gregory Bateson. Bateson, with his work *Mind and Nature*, was trying to find the pattern which connects us back to the nature in a philosophical sense, an idea that had already found popularity among the hippie movement and which was a deliberate attempt to address some of the problems of heroic materialism. Similarly, there were works such as the Gaia hypothesis formulated by James Lovelock and (microbiologist!) Lynn Margulis which also put man within 'nature' as a complex system rather than apart from it. It's strange to think that our reliance on nature had to be explicitly recognised but our attitude to nature has deep roots in western culture and it's not going to be easy to change it.

"We need to get rid of the notion that all natural things are valueless in themselves, merely pretty extras, expendable, either secondary to human purposes or actually pernicious. That notion is so fearfully misleading that we must ditch it somehow, even though we don't yet have a perfectly clear map of the ideals that we shall need to put in its place." (The Myths We Live By, p. 174)

Of course, this doesn't mean over-romanticising nature, which was arguably one of the reasons the romantics and the hippies failed to provide a viable alternative. Somewhere between the blind domination of heroic materialism and a naïve worship of nature there should at least be a place to recognise that we are a part of the planet and not separate from it. In theory, the environmentalist movement of the 20th century was aiming at something like that but it was bought out by financial interests. What counts for the environmental movement these days is nothing more than heroic materialism in disguise. The wind turbines and solar farms are simply the continuation of the bridges and dams and freeways. They are certainly not what was had in mind in the 60s and 70s where the 'small is beautiful' ethic was alive and the focus was on harmonising with nature rather than dominating it.

The other important point to make is that the ideas from systems theory, cybernetics and romanticism are an explicit counterbalance to the high modernist ideology and its single-minded focus. If there was one science that arose in the 20th century as the primary challenger to that ideology it was ecology. Ecology is explicitly concerned with connectedness and relationship. By pointing out the inter-connectedness of things ecology became a way to recognise the second order effects of action which mostly translated into a critique of heroic materialism by pointing to the environmental degradation wrought by corporations pursuing the bottom line. Of course, thinking through the ramifications of an idea is time-consuming and often tedious. The primary advantage of focus is that it allows action but tends to ignore the consequences of action. The primary advantage of de-focus is to bring the consequences to light but in doing so it makes action more difficult. The balance, of course, is somewhere in the middle.

Arguably, the *suave technocracy* was a structure that facilitated that balance by harmonising civil society, democracy and technocracy. Our reversion to vulgar technocracy, initially justified by the plague story, has thrown that balance out. At time of writing, many western societies are still being governed by the technocracy in states of emergency. To the extent that this continues it is going to cause lasting economic damage which is most likely to affect small business and the wage class. In this way, it is civil society itself that is being weakened. This has the potential to throw things out of balance permanently. We may see a lasting reversion to vulgar technocracy. Of course, the primary feedback mechanism is still democracy and any economic impacts will probably feed into the populist politics that has arisen in recent times. To the extent that such politics represents a correction against the technocracy then things may eventually re-establish their balance. If not, then the corona event could represent a shift back toward the high modernist ideology of the 20th century. Only time will tell.

Postscript

I stated right at the start of this book that what I was aiming to do was to present an analysis of the corona event inspired by systems thinking and cybernetics. I have tried to look at the matter through a variety of different lenses including a narrative lens (the plague story), a journalistic/history lens (recounting the actual events that started the plague story), a science lens, a sociological lens, a psychological lens, an economic lens and others. Recall that all of these lenses are just heuristics. They are not definitive, reductionist truths or solid, reproducible cause and effect relationships. That is, in my opinion, the only real way to approach medium number systems or what we might call *the real world*.

Some people may find this approach unsatisfying. In fact, during the corona event we have seen a strong preference among many people for simplistic, faux certainty backed by strong conviction. Our world has become very complex and that complexity itself has led to a kind of background anxiousness and even fear. It is those emotions that drive the desire for certainty and action. I don't know how to address that except to say that it is up to laypeople to question the experts and to question their leaders. If things are not able to be explained to a layperson, then something is wrong. To throw in one final idea from Richard Feynman – if a scientist can't explain their work to a ten-year-old, they don't understand it. Thus, the generalist perspective, the asking of questions that might sound naïve, is actually necessary in a very practical sense. Bad things happen when that perspective is excluded.

For that reason, I'll finish with a quote from another of my favourite books that deals these issues – Gareth Hardin's *Filters Against Folly*.

Layman or expert, each of us is trying to put together a true picture of that indefinable something we call "reality". The world is too complex for our minds to encompass the whole. We must filter the data and arguments that come in to us. Filtration clarifies: that's good. But the clarification is achieved by filtering out – setting aside – part of reality. Different filters clarify – alter – the total picture in different ways. We need to know the characteristics of our filters, their merits and their defects. Only by understanding these will we be able to protect ourselves against the assumptions (conscious or unconscious), the biases and the prejudices, of our experts.

-

References

Chapter 1

1. https://www.cdc.gov/flu/pandemic-resources/basics/about.html
2. https://www.cell.com/cell/fulltext/S0092-8674(20)30610-3
3. https://www.health.gov.au/news/chief-medical-officer-on-sunrise-about-novel-coronavirus

Chapter 2

1. https://www.who.int/news-room/detail/29-06-2020-covid-timeline
2. https://promedmail.org/promed-post/?id=6864153%20#COVID19
3. https://www.cdc.gov/pneumonia/causes.html
4. https://www.thoracic.org/patients/patient-resources/resources/top-pneumonia-facts.pdf
5. https://www.nytimes.com/2020/03/29/world/asia/coronavirus-china.html
6. https://www.health.com/condition/cold-flu-sinus/viral-bacterial-pneumonia
7. http://weekly.chinacdc.cn/en/article/doi/10.46234/ccdcw2020.017

8. https://link.springer.com/content/pdf/10.1007%2Fs00705-012-1583-5.pdf
9. https://www.ncbi.nlm.nih.gov/pmc/articles/PMC7095448/
10. https://www.who.int/csr/don/05-january-2020-pneumonia-of-unkown-cause-china/en/
11. https://www.gisaid.org/about-us/mission/
12. https://www.dzif.de/en/researchers-develop-first-diagnostic-test-novel-coronavirus-china
13. https://www.nejm.org/doi/full/10.1056/NEJMoa2001316
14. https://www.nejm.org/doi/full/10.1056/NEJMoa2001316
15. https://www.who.int/china/news/detail/09-01-2020-who-statement-regarding-cluster-of-pneumonia-cases-in-wuhan-china
16. https://www.eurosurveillance.org/content/10.2807/1560-7917.ES.2020.25.3.2000045#html_fulltext
17. https://apps.who.int/iris/bitstream/handle/10665/163636/WHO_HSE_FOS_15.1_eng.pdf
18. https://www.cochrane.org/news/featured-review-can-symptoms-and-medical-examination-accurately-diagnose-covid-19-disease
19. https://www.news.com.au/technology/science/human-body/australian-scientists-grow-coronavirus-in-a-laboratory/news-story/e4b20ced324b6fbec99402ce2255b873
20. https://en.wikipedia.org/wiki/Replication_crisis#Overall
21. https://www.ncbi.nlm.nih.gov/pmc/articles/PMC2937520/

Chapter 3

1. https://www.youtube.com/watch?v=SwlkumcRf6w
2. https://www.cdc.gov/sars/clinical/guidance.html
3. https://wwwn.cdc.gov/nndss/conditions/coronavirus-disease-2019-covid-19/case-definition/2020/08/05/
4. https://theinfectiousmyth.com/book/SARS.pdf

5. https://www.doherty.edu.au/news-events/news/the-positives-and-negatives-of-mass-testing-for-coronavirus
6. https://jcm.asm.org/content/jcm/51/1/2.full.pdf

Chapter 4

1. https://www.cdc.gov/flu/pandemic-resources/basics/about.html
2. https://www.researchsquare.com/article/rs-35331/v1
3. https://www.theage.com.au/national/can-i-catch-it-from-my-friend-s-pencil-talking-to-kids-about-covid-19-20200828-p55qao.html
4. https://www.npr.org/2020/04/14/834109166/where-did-the-coronavirus-originate-virus-hunters-find-genetic-clues-in-bats
5. https://www.thelancet.com/journals/lancet/article/PIIS0140-6736(20)30418-9/fulltext
6. https://www.sciencedaily.com/releases/2020/04/200401111657.htm
7. https://www.nature.com/articles/d41586-017-07766-9#ref-CR2
8. https://www.nature.com/articles/nm.3985
9. https://www.ecohealthalliance.org/financials-strategy
10. https://www.independentsciencenews.org/commentaries/a-proposed-origin-for-sars-cov-2-and-the-covid-19-pandemic/

Chapter 5

1. https://apps.who.int/iris/bitstream/handle/10665/259834/WER9302.pdf?sequence=1
2. https://www.nejm.org/doi/full/10.1056/NEJMoa2001017
3. https://en.wikipedia.org/wiki/Koch's_postulates

4. https://nyaspubs.onlinelibrary.wiley.com/doi/abs/10.1111/j.1749-6632.1957.tb46066.x
5. https://www.nationalgeographic.com/science/phenomena/2013/02/20/an-infinity-of-viruses/
6. https://www.inverse.com/article/49747-what-is-the-human-virome
7. https://www.sciencedirect.com/science/article/pii/S1879625711001908?via%3Dihub
8. https://www.ncbi.nlm.nih.gov/pmc/articles/PMC3519536/
9. https://www.bmj.com/content/356/bmj.j831
10. https://www.ncbi.nlm.nih.gov/pmc/articles/PMC7107506/
11. https://onlinelibrary.wiley.com/doi/epdf/10.1002/jmv.2161
12. https://jcm.asm.org/content/jcm/49/7/2631.full.pdf
13. https://onlinelibrary.wiley.com/doi/full/10.1002/ppul.21552
14. https://cmr.asm.org/content/cmr/9/1/18.full.pdf
15. https://www.gla.ac.uk/news/headline_703609_en.html
16. https://cmr.asm.org/content/cmr/9/1/18.full.pdf

Chapter 6

1. https://www.worldstarhiphop.com/videos/video.php?v=wshh31z5zOX10E1HM85l

Chapter 7

1. https://www.fs.fed.us/nrs/pubs/jrnl/2014/nrs_2014_stevens_001.pdf
2. https://www.childrenandnature.org/2017/11/15/biophobia-on-raising-a-generation-of-nature-phobic-kids/
3. https://www.webmd.com/parenting/features/kids-and-dirt-germs#1

Chapter 8

1. https://www.thelancet.com/journals/lancet/article/PIIS0140-6736(08)61022-3/fulltext

Chapter 10

1. https://www.thelancet.com/journals/lancet/article/PIIS0140-6736(08)61022-3/fulltext
2. http://environmentalhistory.org/20th-century/cold-war-1950-59/
3. https://www.ncbi.nlm.nih.gov/pmc/articles/PMC4024220/

www.ingramcontent.com/pod-product-compliance
Ingram Content Group UK Ltd.
Pitfield, Milton Keynes, MK11 3LW, UK
UKHW020659070726
13598UKWH00011B/100

9 780648 948612